PASSIVE
PROSPECTING

PASSIVE
PROSPECTING

DOMINATE YOUR MARKET
WITHOUT COLD CALLING, CHASING CLIENTS,
OR SPENDING MONEY ON ADS

LEVI LASCSAK & TRAVIS PLUMB

FOREWORD BY RYAN SERHANT

LIONCREST
PUBLISHING

Passive Prospecting

Dominate Your Market without Cold Calling, Chasing Clients, or Spending Money on Ads

FIRST EDITION

ISBN 978-1-5445-3810-5 Hardcover
      978-1-5445-3808-2 Paperback
      978-1-5445-3809-9 Ebook
      978-1-5445-3811-2 Audiobook

Dedicated to my parents, friends, and mentors,

who have all been an influence in my life.

—LEVI LASCSAK

To my wife Sam and my beautiful children,

my friends, my mentors who have been there along the way

to transform my life—and to all those who wish to

take their life and business to another level, knowing there is

a better, smarter way to make an impact, change lives,

and make a lot of money passively.

—TRAVIS PLUMB

CONTENTS

PART 1
PASSIVE PROSPECTING PRINCIPLES

PART 2
PASSIVE PROSPECTING PROCESS

FOREWORD

PASSIVE PROSPECTING

RYAN SERHANT, CEO OF SERHANT

There was a time in my career when I felt like I would be stuck doing $2,000 rentals for recent NYU grads who had just landed their first jobs FOREVER. Just a decade later I'm the CEO of SERHANT. We closed nearly $1.45 billion in sales last year, and this year we're going to hit over two billion. How did I go from renting cheap apartments to dozens of people named Emily (I swear every NYU grad was named Emily back then) to the CEO of the most recognized real estate brand in the world?

I made a YouTube video.

Seriously. It was that simple.

You see, I didn't want to sit back and wait for business that was never going to come. I wanted to take action and create a lucrative business for the future version of myself. When Future

Ryan found out that the founder of the Discovery Channel had just put his ranch in Colorado on the market for $280 million, he took action. I reached out to the broker and asked if I could come to Colorado and film content for YouTube. He said, "Sure, whatever you want, but I'm not paying for it." "No problem," I said. "We'll pay for it."

I flew all the way out there, made a three-part YouTube video about the ranch and put it out into the world. It was a winning scenario for both sides. For him, the exposure was an answer to the question high-end clients always ask, "Why aren't you doing more to sell my mansion?" For me, it was an opportunity to associate myself with a nine-figure listing.

Fast-forward in time. A kid in the Middle East whose dad is a multibillionaire sees the video.

This kid's dad happens to have a Park Avenue penthouse he wants to sell. Their representative reaches out to me and suddenly I'm selling their $170 million apartment. They didn't find me because I'm the greatest salesperson in the world; they found me because I made a video that associated my brand with listings at that price point. All of this happened because of my YouTube video! I didn't think of that YouTube video as passive prospecting. That's a name Levi and Travis came up with on their own. But what I did is just what Levi and Travis describe in this book: I created YouTube videos that brought the kind of clients I was looking for to *me*.

You can take it from me. The mindset and process Levi and Travis describe works. The principles and practical guidance they offer in this book aren't limited to real estate. The principles can help transform any business…and your life along with it. So, what are you waiting for? Why not become the future you now? Read this book. Buy a copy for a friend. Check out their YouTube channel, "Living in Dallas Texas." If you ever have a chance to see them on stage, go for it. You need to keep your eye on these guys. They're blowing things up.

INTRODUCTION

THE POWER OF PASSIVE PROSPECTING

In my first month in the real estate business in Dallas, Texas, December of 2020, my partner, Travis Plumb, and I sold zero homes. It was the same for the first quarter of 2021: zero homes. But in April of 2021, we closed our first two transactions.

It wasn't a lot, but it was something.

Then things changed—in a big way.

Over the next fifteen months, we generated 1,696 leads that produced 217 transactions, a conversion rate of 13 percent. We did over $121 million in sales volume and generated more than $3.6 million in commissions.

Throughout that time, there's one number that stayed at zero: our ad spend. We didn't make a single cold call, knock on a single door, or send out a single postcard.

And the odds were stacked against us. Between us, Travis and I had decades of experience in sales but none in real estate. There were nearly 12,000 active real estate agents in Dallas in 2020, many of them well established; we were new and unknown. According to the National Association of Realtors, 87 percent of agents fail in two years or less; maybe that's because the average annual income of an agent with no experience in their first two years is $8,800.[1]

How'd we do it?

By making YouTube videos that provided people researching information with the answers they were looking for. We didn't have to chase clients, because our videos brought clients to us. There are days when it feels like our business is building itself.

From our years of experience in selling everything from gym memberships to cars to retirement plans, Travis and I knew sales as a rejection-based business. We both loved sales, but we hated prospecting—and that's where we spent almost all of our time.

Passive prospecting through YouTube videos set us free. That alone shows the power of passive prospecting. And no matter what you're selling, we believe it can set you free too.

Everyone we know loves the idea of passive income—money that keeps coming in with little or no effort on your part. We

---

[1] "Highlights from the NAR Member Profile," National Association of Realtors, July 11, 2022, https://www.nar.realtor/research-and-statistics/research-reports/highlights -from-the-nar-member-profile#income.

sure do. Well, when it comes to bringing in customers, passive prospecting works the same way.

Maybe that sounds too good to be true. It's not!

WHO WE ARE

I've been responsible for developing our YouTube marketing strategy, and I've created most of our videos. So the book is written in my voice, but the success we're describing in it is ours together. Travis is the ultimate closer—and make no mistake about it, we're full partners. Neither of us would be where we are today without the other. We're both from small towns in Texas and are veterans who served in combat in Iraq. We've both experienced great success in sales—and seen it taken away by forces beyond our control overnight. We've both had to start over more than once, and we've both had dark days.

We approached real estate knowing how hard it is for new agents—or any business owner—to get established at the beginning of their journey, and how often they fail no matter how hard they work. So we took a different approach. We both knew marketing was the key to success, and I dove deep into exploring the options. As I'll explain later in the book, that research led us to YouTube—and we haven't looked back since. Our approach has enabled us to build a team that frees each of us to give 100 percent of our effort to what we do best.

The results we've achieved tell you all you need to know about how well it's worked.

WHAT YOU'LL DISCOVER

This book is divided into two parts.

PART 1

In Part 1, I'll lay out the principles of passive prospecting. Building a successful YouTube marketing strategy is a matter of applying them. Part 1 is your foundation, laying out the power of YouTube and showing why it's the best platform to generate high-quality, top-tier clients who are dying to do business with you instead of your competitors.

Interruption versus Intention-Based Marketing. *Interruption marketing puts your message in front of someone who's trying to do something else. Intention-based YouTube marketing puts your message in front of someone who's searching for answers.*

Quantity versus Quality. *A marketing strategy based on lead quantity takes more time, effort, and money than a YouTube strategy based on lead quality.*

Paid versus Free. *A paid marketing strategy buys leads. A free marketing strategy using YouTube videos brings customers who've already decided they want to work with you at no cost.*

Seasonal versus Evergreen. *Seasonal content is temporary.*

Evergreen content is relevant day after day, week after week, month after month, year after year.

Selfish versus Service. *Traditional marketing is about selling yourself. Service-based marketing that provides answers people are searching for will bring grateful customers to you.*

Short Form versus Long Form. *Short-form videos may seem like the best way to match shrinking attention spans. But long-form videos build relationships that lead to business.*

Local versus Global Reach. *YouTube marketing can help you own a local market—while also bringing you customers anywhere, anytime, from all around the globe.*

Take Time versus Make Time. *Making YouTube videos doesn't take you time. It makes you time. Better still, it compounds your time—creating opportunities no other platform can match.*

Active versus Passive Prospecting. *Active prospecting is rejection-based and doesn't scale. Passive prospecting brings business to you—and it never stops working, without rejection or bugging your friends and family to do business with you.*

PART 2

In Part 2, I'll lay out the process of building a marketing strategy based on YouTube videos. It's more than enough to get you started on the path to success too. This is the how-to section of the book, laying out how to do what we did—but for your business.

Channel Buildout. *How your YouTube channel looks and how it's structured will have a significant effect on how easy it is for searchers to find you, the first impressions they form, and what they're likely to do next.*

Content Creation. *Deciding what videos to make and how to title them doesn't have to be a matter of guesswork—and making videos is easier than you think.*

Optimization. *A great video won't boost your business if searchers can't find it. Dialing in the backend search engine optimization and filling in every blank will help YouTube find your audience for you.*

Lead Conversion. *Customer Relations Management (CRM) software is essential in guiding customers from contact to conversion —and doing it at scale through automation.*

Adjusting to Change (and YouTube Shorts). *As YouTube Shorts make clear, platforms change—and you need to change with them. Be strategic, test your assumptions, and let experiments point the way.*

WE'RE HERE TO HELP

You have to choose your *hard* in life.

It's hard working out. But after serving in Iraq and returning with a digestive disease, I learned it's a lot harder being sick.

It's hard owning a business—but to me, it's a lot harder having a job.

And it's hard making YouTube videos—but to me, it's a lot harder making calls.

I'll also say this: at this point, no one has to convince me to keep making YouTube videos.

In 2021, our first year in real estate, we closed $1 million in commissions off of 160 YouTube videos. That was our marketing; it's all we did. And that's like getting paid $6,250 a video.

Think about it. If I offered you $6,250 to make a YouTube video, wouldn't you do it?

In the first half of 2022, our second year, we made $2.6 million in commissions off of fifty-six videos. That's like making almost $47,000 a video.

I don't know many people who wouldn't leap at the chance to make $47,000 just for recording a YouTube video!

Now, those are our numbers. Of course we can't guarantee that passive prospecting will bring you the same success in real estate or whatever business you're in. But we've written this book in the hope of providing you with enough information to take your best shot, by developing your own passive prospecting strategy through YouTube videos.

We're believers, because passive prospecting has changed our lives. We hope after reading this book it will change yours too.

PART 1

PASSIVE PROSPECTING PRINCIPLES

CHAPTER 1

INTERRUPTION VERSUS INTENTION-BASED MARKETING

Digital marketing experts say that most Americans are exposed to 6,000 to 10,000 ads every day.[2] Think about that. How is it even possible?

It's because we're conducting most of our marketing by interruption—and it never stops. We've been exposed to this our entire lives. Ads are everywhere, on everything, every day. TV

---

[2] Sam Carr, "How Many Ads Do We See a Day in 2022?", Lunio, February 15, 2021, https://lunio.ai/blog/strategy/how-many-ads-do-we-see-a-day/.

commercials. Billboards. On TikTok, Facebook, and Instagram. In magazines. (Ads take up half the pages!) Even through our phones. Ever gotten a call about your car warranty?

Clearly, we're not buying 6,000 to 10,000 products every single day. No one is even in the market for 10,000 products, and most of us aren't necessarily in the market for a particular product when we see an ad for it. Most of the time, the ads coming at us interrupt us when we're trying to do something else.

That's why it's called interruption marketing. Most businesses have been marketing this way for the longest time. None of us can escape it. But when you hear "interruption," what's the first thing that comes to your mind? It's probably the fact that you don't like to be interrupted.

I was driving by a small sports complex the other day. There may have been thirty different advertisements displayed on the outside. T-Mobile, Nike, and Puma were all sponsoring that building, and along with everyone else on the building they were trying to get my attention in the one second it took me to go past the complex.

At one level, it works. People can process an image in thirteen milliseconds,[3] so I had time to take them all in. (Thirteen milliseconds is much faster than the blink of an eye, and it's why

---

[3] Anne Trafton, "In the blink of an eye," MIT News, January 16, 2014, https://news .mit.edu/2014/in-the-blink-of-an-eye-0116.

thumbnails are so important on YouTube. More on that later!)

But seeing an ad isn't everything. I already have a T-Mobile cell phone. So whenever I see a T-Mobile ad, it's really irrelevant to me—unless they were to have a brand-new phone or something like that. But I would probably know that ahead of time. I don't need to wait for T-Mobile's advertising.

Nobody says, hey, I need to buy some soap—I'm going to go check out Facebook. No one driving around town needs the trial lawyer they'll see on a dozen billboards—unless they get in a car wreck while they're looking at the billboard. No one goes on TikTok to see if they can find a dancing plumber. No one who just bought a six-pack of soap on Amazon needs to see a soap ad every time they go on Facebook to catch up on the news. No one goes on YouTube or Netflix or sits in front of the TV specifically to watch the ads.

There's so much interruption marketing that it leaves advertisers trying even harder to get our attention. That's why fashion magazines have bright-colored ads and perfume ads you can scratch and sniff. That's why jingles and slogans were invented. How many times have you heard a jingle once or twice—and then it's stuck in your head for the rest of the day? You could probably recite jingles from your childhood, even though the products or services may not even still be around. If I were to say, "Like a good neighbor…" you could probably finish the sentence. Does that mean you're going to drop everything and buy insurance?

Think about commercials during Christmas. I always see a commercial for a Lexus with a big red bow on it. Every year, somebody's giving away that car as a Christmas gift. How many times have you seen that ad? And how many people who see it run out and buy that Lexus? Probably not a lot. But if you see that commercial every single year, stemming from childhood, maybe it gets embedded. Maybe that's even the reason you own a Lexus today! It must work—but it could take weeks, months, even years before you buy.

That's the ultimate goal of interruption marketing: to hit you over the head so many times, over and over and over again, that finally, when you're in the market for that product or service, that jingle will come through or you'll recognize that brand from the commercials you've seen hundreds of times before. To win with interruption marketing, you have to retarget the buyer over and over and over again—and pay for it every single time. That's why it's usually the people with the biggest budget who win in the end. It's also why many businesses fail so quickly: they run out of money.

Most of the time, though, interruption marketing just gets in our way. When a football game is on, I want to watch the game. (Unless it's the Super Bowl. That's the only time I can think of when people are saying, "Hey, I can't wait to watch the ads!") What do you typically do during commercials? You go to the bathroom. You grab something to eat. You check your phone to stay up to date. You may even change the channel, flipping back and forth between shows. That's why streaming services can charge a premium for an ad-free experience.

It's the same thing with social media platforms. There's nothing wrong with Facebook, Instagram, or TikTok. In the real estate business, we met a lot of agents who were successful on all of them. But they're also interruption platforms. As far as I know, not a lot of people say, "Let's go on Instagram and see if we can find the best real estate agent," when it's time to buy a house.

Can a real estate agent establish a brand by marketing on those platforms? Absolutely. But you're left hoping that six months, twelve months, or eighteen months down the road, when they are in the market to buy or sell a home, they will think about you. According to one analysis, it can actually take up to twenty-four months for an online real estate lead to convert, and the national average conversion rate for online real estate leads is typically reported to be between 2 and 3 percent. That means you've got to talk to a hundred people before you close one or two deals. That's a lot of work. (The reality may be even worse. The National Association of Realtors has put the figure between 0.4 and 1.2 percent.)[4]

---

[4] Joanna Harrison, "How Long Does it Take to Convert Online Real Estate Leads?", BoomTown!, March 21, 2022, https://resources.boomtownroi.com/blog/how-long -does-it-take-to-convert-online-real-estate-leads.

INTENTION-BASED MARKETING

Let's say you see a dog food commercial ten times a day. That doesn't mean you're going to run out and buy dog food. Someone's paying to show you those ads whether you're in the market for dog food today or not.

But when you pour out that last bowl of dog food, you definitely don't want Fluffy to die, right?

What are you likely to do?

Well, if there's a little left in the bag, you might go on Amazon—and search "dog food." You'll probably find it within seconds of your search, especially if you bought it before—and you'll buy it. It'll be on your doorstep within two days. If that's too long, you'll go to the store, head for the dog food aisle, and search there.

Either way, you've got the *intention* to buy dog food. You don't need marketing to tell you to do it. You don't need a billboard. You don't need a TV commercial. You don't need somebody to send you a postcard to tell you that you just ran out of dog food. You know that you need it—or else. So you go and buy it.

Now think about this: As a small business owner, what if you could get in front of people when they have full intention? When they're in research mode, looking to buy (or sell), searching for a solution to their problem?

That's intention-based marketing.

It's kind of like fishing—but with an expert guide. Fish tend to feed in certain areas at certain times of the day. They tend to respond to certain lures. If you go with an expert guide who knows the area, you're going to reel them in all day long. It's a lot better than going out there on your own and just guessing.

With intention-based marketing, you know exactly who you're trying to target, and you know exactly what they are searching for. And all you have to do is put the information they need in front of them. Maybe you've heard this question: What's the most important thing if you're going to open a food stand? Most people might say great food or a great location. The correct answer is a starving audience, because if you have a starving audience, it doesn't really matter where you're located or even if your food is all that great.

With intention-based marketing, you don't have to go looking for customers; they'll come to you. We guarantee you that if you're a plumber, there's someone in your market right now who's searching for a plumber. You name the business, we'll guarantee it. Financial services. Interior decorating. A new car. A used car. A mechanic. Dog grooming. Dog training. Even food for Fluffy.

They're going onto Google and YouTube and are intentionally searching for information in your marketplace. If you're in real estate, like we are, whether you live in Dallas, like we do, or Phoenix, Denver, Minneapolis, or Washington, DC, there are people right now who are looking to move to your area, and they're searching. They're looking for answers. And they're probably not saying, "Hey, honey, it's time to buy a house. Let's go on Facebook and see what's on the market." If they're relocating, they don't even know an agent—and they're not even looking for one at first. They want to know what it's like to live there.

A searcher with intent doesn't need to see an advertisement ten, twenty, or a hundred times to make their choice. They're in research mode. And they're likely to choose from one of the first three to five options they see in their search results. More than a quarter of people are actually going to click on the first result![5] They understand that a ranking at the top gives validation that it's probably a good product or service. Maybe you've heard the joke: Where's the best place to hide a dead body? It's on the second page of a Google or Amazon search result.

There's truth in that joke. When's the last time you actually clicked to go to the second page of Amazon? Most of the time, you're going to find what you need on that first page. Amazon rankings are based on reviews, sales, and a lot of other factors, but many sellers actually pay per click to improve the ranking of their products. The small business owners on Amazon want to be on the first page, because that's where all the eyeballs are.

---

[5] Matt G. Southern, "Over 25% of People Click the First Google Search Result," *Search Engine Journal*, https://www.searchenginejournal.com/google-first-page -clicks/374516/#close.

They don't have to win every click. If they can just get a small percentage of them, they can have a very successful product.

But what if you could get what you offer in front of searchers looking for answers organically? We can help you with that challenge—and our solution begins with YouTube.

WHY YOUTUBE?

When people are looking to kill some time while they're in line at Chick-fil-A, they'll go on Facebook. Their attention span is short. They're looking for diversions. But when they're seeking out information, they're going to Google, the world's most-used search engine, and YouTube (which is owned by Google), the second most-used search engine—and their attention spans are long.

That makes YouTube the perfect place to be. The metrics show why.

Let's start with search frequency. Plano, Texas, is a suburb outside Dallas. Last time we looked, it got 90,500 monthly searches on Google. And on YouTube, it got 834,000 searches. Why? Because people who are interested in Plano don't just want to read about it. They want to see it.

Our channel analytics paint their own picture.

Globally, more than 80 percent of internet users use a mobile device to surf the web. Ninety-five percent of Facebook traffic comes from mobile devices.[6] Mobile devices are also responsible for 70 percent of all watch time on YouTube.

Our figures are different. Only 47 percent of traffic to our YouTube channel comes from mobile. Most of it—53 percent—comes from TV, computers, and tablets.

Why? Remember: Our videos provide viewers who have questions—viewers with intent, doing research—with the information they're searching for. Questions such as, "What are the best Dallas suburbs?" Or "What are the pros and cons of living in Plano, Texas?" And TVs, computers, and tablets are research devices. They are get-comfortable devices. You sit on your couch, you sit at your desk or in your favorite chair—and you dig in. It's time to research; you're in the mindset to consume long-form content. Almost 29 percent of our traffic in 2021 came from TVs. Think about how powerful that is. People were sitting on their couch, or possibly lying in their bed, watching our videos.

They are locked in too. Our average view-duration on TV was more than nine and a half minutes. On mobile, it was four and a half. Two-thirds of our total watch time was on TV, computer, or tablets—compared to only one-third on mobile. (Why? Well, your phone is limited. If you've ever tried to buy something on your phone, or search for something, or save it to watch

---

[6] Aleksandar S., "What Percentage of Internet Traffic Is Mobile in 2022?", TechJury, updated June 8, 2022, https://techjury.net/blog/what-percentage-of-internet-traffic-is-mobile/.

later when you've got more time, you know it can be a little too complicated.)

For YouTube, watch time is the most important metric. The longer someone is on their platform, the more money they can make from advertising. If someone watches one of our videos, that's going to trigger YouTube to serve them another one. (We all know this is true, because we've all made the mistake of watching a silly cat video—and our YouTube feeds are filled with silly cat videos for the next thirty days.)

Our average time of contact to contract is forty-seven days, which is amazing by our industry's standards. But we've done deals within six, eighteen, twenty-four hours of people reaching out to us—because they have full intentionality. We don't have to sell ourselves to them. The fastest we've ever put anyone under contract from first contact is three hours. That happened because in one of our videos, I mentioned that we don't lose deals. This client had just lost her sixth offer with a different agent. She called us based on that video, with a specific address, and asked if we would put our money where our mouth was and get this house under contract for her. It took us only three hours to do it.

That's the power of intention-based marketing. It worked for us in real estate—and it can work for your small business too.

Interruption versus Intention-Based Marketing Takeaway

Interruption marketing puts your message in front of someone who's trying to do something else. Intention-based marketing puts your message in front of someone who's looking for what you offer.

When you know their intention, you'll have their attention.

CHAPTER 2

QUANTITY VERSUS QUALITY

Here's the question anyone who's trying to sell something faces: Would you rather have a lot of leads, which keeps you busy, or fewer leads and a higher conversion rate? It's a question of quantity versus quality. Most people we know come down on the side of quality. That's where we come down too—and YouTube videos have done more than any other form of marketing we've ever tried to bring us the high-quality leads we value.

We've both pursued lead quantity strategies at earlier stages in our careers—and it was costly and tiring. We'll start by exploring why.

CHASING QUANTITY

You could spend $10 a day on Facebook ads, about $300 a month, and on average collect about one hundred leads per month. That's pretty good—but that's also one hundred people to call.

Travis has pursued this strategy in real estate, and others we've worked with have too. We're not saying that it doesn't work; you can be successful with it. Facebook ads were one of Travis's biggest sources of leads. Facebook is good at capturing information from people; all it takes is a couple of clicks for the user to give permission, whether they realize it or not. And Travis found himself spending hours every day in conversations with a lot of people who weren't necessarily even in the market. Most didn't know who he was, or they didn't remember what they clicked on or filled out. He'd hear things like, "Is this about that real estate ad? Yeah, I just liked the picture," or "I was just curious about the price of that home." Sometimes he'd even hear, "Who is this again?"

A reminder: Along with Instagram and TikTok, Facebook is an interruption platform. Not many people are going there because they're in the market for a home, a car, an electrician, or financial advice.

You do get to talk to a lot of people, and you can build a big database of contacts. In the next month, you'll collect another hundred leads, and in the month after that too. Over three months, you'll get three hundred people in that database.

From a quantity standpoint, that's great. Three hundred people in three months! But now you've got three hundred people you need to call just to maintain a relationship. They still may not be looking to buy or sell a home.

The struggle only gets harder. As every month passes, you add more leads. Eight months in, you're at eight hundred leads. There's no way you can keep up with all those people on a monthly basis—and that leads you to build in triggers, automations, and retargeting campaigns. Most Customer Relationship Management (CRM) systems have those capabilities, so it's doable. But you're going to have to go through a lot of people, and you'll have to spend a lot of money to do it.

THE TOP OF THE FUNNEL

Here's another issue with focusing on the quantity of leads: they typically start at the top of the sales funnel. That's a marketing term for describing the sales process. There's the top of the funnel, middle of the funnel, and bottom of the funnel—which is where the sales process or client journey ends.

People at the top of the sales funnel don't really know who you are. They're just seeing you, your ad, or your product or service for the very first time. They might not even remember you when you call the next day. They're not familiar with you yet.

That's what leads marketers to target custom or lookalike audiences on Facebook and other social media platforms. It also leads to retargeting campaigns to hit people again and again and again until you build that familiarity and you can move them to the middle of the sales funnel.

Remember: all you're building is familiarity. It's not a relationship until you move them to the very bottom of the funnel. You can call them at any point in the funnel, but you're not in the best place to capture them until they're at the bottom. Only then do you have your best chance of converting that lead.

It adds up to a lot of time, effort, and money.

But what if you could start at the bottom of the funnel and do it with less time, effort, and money?

You can, if you use YouTube videos and develop *quality* leads. We've found that makes it much easier to get what everyone who's selling something wants: conversions.

QUALITY LEADS

As people search and find your videos on their own, they're actually moving themselves through the sales process, down the sales funnel, along the client journey—whatever you want to call it. They're walking themselves through that process. And as they consume multiple videos, they become more familiar with you.

This is where they become middle-of-the-funnel leads. They're starting to know you and trust you, and they're actually starting to develop a relationship with you. Once they reach out, when they make that phone call, they've moved themselves to the bottom of the funnel. Until they call, you're not even aware they exist—and when you hear from them, they're ready to do business with you. That's a quality lead. Facebook and other forms of marketing can deliver *more* leads—but when it comes to quality leads, less can be more.

Better still, quality leads do that work on their own, at no cost to you. They're completely bought in because they've done it themselves. They're in control of their own choices. That's a very powerful way to do business. It pretty much removes all the selling from the process. When we get a call from a potential client, we don't really have to convince them to work with us, or pitch them on why we're the best agents to help them out. They've already made that determination for themselves through the videos we created and the content they watched.

That's the best thing about utilizing a free strategy through YouTube: you're going to attract a much more qualified client.

Yes, you can pay to put your ads in front of people on other platforms, and you'll only be charged if they click on your ad. Could they be a motivated buyer or seller? Yes. But even if they are, there's no relationship there. Regardless, you still have to give them a call.

You can also turn to Google Pay Per Click Ads. They're only shown to people searching for what your business offers. Their Local Services Ads even enable searchers to call in and get directly in touch with you. But you still have to develop a relationship, build rapport, and establish credibility. That is difficult to do in a short amount of time.

You could develop a lead capture system to feed that database, putting out free reports or guides or other downloads in exchange for their phone number and email. We don't have one, but we could test it. We would collect a lot of data and see if we could convert some of the people who sign up. But they may just want that free download. They may just want that free report. They may not actually be in the market for another three, six, or nine months. Yes, we'd capture their information, but we'd be in pursuit mode. That's not a position we want to be in.

It's why a lot of people fail out of real estate, or out of sales in general: It's a rejection business. We hear people talk about this all the time: "Hey, we're in a rejection business, right? You have to get through nine no's to get to one yes."

That's just not the case in our business. We don't really get any no's. We don't get calls from people who don't want to work with us. Remember, our average time from contact to contract is forty-seven days, an amazing figure in our industry. The people who see our videos and don't want to work with us don't call.

We don't even know they're out there—and we're not chasing after people, pursuing or calling them either. We just create the content, provide the value, and wait for the business to come in. We're not spending months following up with people, chasing them down, sending out information, or keeping in touch. And if we did, who knows? We could end up ruining that relationship versus strengthening it over time.

CONTROLLING THE LEAD FLOW

One good thing about paying for lead sources is that it should be controllable. If you spend $10, $20, or $30 a day, you should be able to anticipate that each level is going to produce a predictable, increasing number of leads. If you stop spending, your lead generation stops too. You can also measure your conversion rate. If you're going to pay for ads, that's the only way to know whether it's worth it. We like to say that you should never have a marketing budget. You should have a testing budget. Once your testing budget determines how to turn dimes into dollars, you should spend as much as possible!

In real estate, if it takes you $10,000 worth of leads to sell a $300,000 home for a $9,000 commission, then you might want to consider another lead source. But if you spend $3,000 and you close a $9,000 commission, you should want to spend $3,000 all day long: spend three, net six, rinse and repeat. It's important to measure home by home. You should be able to say, "I closed this one home by spending $3,000."

If you're generating quality leads organically through YouTube, the only way to control the lead flow is through the number of videos you publish. When we started out, the real estate agents in Dallas who were publishing on YouTube posted one video per week—so we posted three. But if you're a solo agent—or in another business—and you don't have ambitions to expand to a team or hire more help, then you could back off on content. The results may not be instantaneous. It may take a few months before you see a change. And it doesn't always work; you could have a video take off on you and return way more views—and leads—than you were expecting.

At the end of 2021, starting with a video we published on Thanksgiving Day, almost every video we published took off right out of the gate. We backed off on content production, because we hadn't seen that before. We wanted to step back, evaluate, and try to understand what was happening. But in the first quarter of 2022, the calls kept coming.

In late summer of 2022, we had our most views ever—but we were down in leads. Why? Well, it's the end of summer; everyone's going back to school, and families are disrupted. And the market's changing. We're not seeing an uptick in new clients, but we are seeing an uptick in clients we worked with six to twelve months ago who wanted to wait and let the market settle before making a move.

It's an inexact science, because it's an organic process, and our videos aren't the only factor that influences the decisions people make. But what's been consistent is the quality of the leads we see.

GETTING RESULTS

We get calls from new clients every day. Our conversion rate over our first eighteen months in business was 13 percent, and as we've said, our average time from contact to contract was forty-seven days. That's exceptional—about ten times the rate you might expect Facebook ads to yield in that short amount of time. We've had to talk to a lot fewer people. And remember: all our business is inbound, not outbound. Our clients initiate the call, text, email, or Zoom session. They're qualified and motivated.

That's the difference a strategy built around quality over quantity of leads can make.

Quantity versus Quality Takeaway

A marketing strategy based on lead quantity can work, but it takes more time, effort, and money than a strategy based on lead quality that brings motivated, intention-based clients to you.

CHAPTER 3

PAID VERSUS FREE

Most small businesses fail. About 32 percent don't survive their first two years, according to the Small Business Administration. Half are gone within five years.[7] Why? The most common reason is the most basic: they run out of cash.[8]

In our business, the numbers are worse: Remember, 87 percent of real estate agents fail within the first two years. Why is that? Most of the time, it's not because they're bad people. It's not because they're bad agents either.

It's usually because they're not effective at lead generation.

---

[7] Patricia Schaefer, "Why Small Businesses Fail: Top 8 Reasons for Startup Failure," ZenBusiness.com, September 1, 2022, https://www.zenbusiness.com/blog/why-small-businesses-fail/.

[8] Katherine Gustafson, "The Percentage of Businesses that Fail and How To Boost Your Chances of Success," LendingTree.com, May 2, 2022, https://www.lendingtree.com/business/small/failure-rate/.

Depending on friends and family for leads isn't typically a big enough sphere of influence. Some people have been very successful doing that, but a majority struggle. And most of the time they come in without a lot of money; we've seen statistics that indicate the average agent gets into the business with less than $5,000 to their name. Because they're very limited on cash, new agents typically lean toward free marketing: their time, energy, and effort. That's why they get into cold calling, door knocking, and calling FSBOs or Expireds on top of working their sphere of influence because all that takes their time versus costing them money.

Does it work? Look at the statistics. Not often enough. The National Association of Realtors says that agents with less than two years experience have an average income of $8,800 a year.[9] (I don't know about you, but I can't live off of $8,800 a year.) Most small businesses face the same dynamic, especially when they're starting out: they need to bring customers in the door, and they don't have much money to spend on advertising to bring them in.

We can speak from experience. If you don't have a significant budget, then it's very hard to gain momentum with paid advertising. Just like with anything in business, you have to be consistent in advertising to generate a significant quantity of

---

[9] "Highlights from the NAR Member Profile," National Association of Realtors, July 11, 2022, https://www.nar.realtor/research-and-statistics/research-reports/highlights-from-the-nar-member-profile#income.

leads. If you've only got a couple thousand dollars to spend, you have to be very, very strategic in choosing what you spend it on. A lot of people default to Facebook or TikTok ads. They *can* be effective. I've got several friends who've been very successful advertising on these platforms. But as we discussed in Chapter 1, social media like Facebook, Instagram, TikTok, and LinkedIn are interruption platforms when it comes to advertising. People aren't typically in a shopping mindset when they go on them.

You can target people with ads, but that doesn't necessarily mean they're in the market when they see your ad. They're scrolling on their feed, checking in on their friends and their family, seeing what people ate for lunch today or watching those cat videos—whatever it is, that's what they're there to consume. They may see your ad. They may even be interested or intrigued enough to click on it—and Facebook has some pretty good ad strategies to capture information very quickly from the people who click. That means you can easily collect a lot of leads from paid advertising. It also explains why Facebook conversion rates are low. The average is about 9 percent, but they vary dramatically by industry; the conversion rate for fitness content is high, at 14 percent, but retail, travel, and hospitality are very low, around 3 percent.[10] In real estate, the short-term conversion rate is only

---

[10] "4 Facebook Ad Benchmarks Across Various Industries," Growth Marketing Genie, https://growthmarketinggenie.com/blog/facebook-ad-benchmarks-across-various -industries-2021/.

1 to 1.5 percent every month—and it can take nine months for a Facebook lead to come to a decision. That means you may have to make a hundred calls to get that one person who is really interested in moving forward in the buying process.

It's a tough way to build your business.

THE PAY-TO-PLAY CHALLENGE

The platforms we've been talking about are typically pay to play: they want businesses to pay them money to promote the content they post. On average, your Facebook post reaches only about 5 percent of your audience organically when you post something.[11] That's why when you post something and you ask your mom, "Hey, did you see my post last night?", or "Didn't you see my post? I was just talking about this last night on Facebook" the answer is often no. Facebook wants you to pay to push that post out, even to your closest friends and family members.

Your posts on Facebook, Instagram, or TikTok don't have a long life either. Typically, they've reached the number of people they're going to reach within twenty-four to forty-eight hours. If you get some virality, you can get a lot of views within the first day or two. But mostly, after that point, it doesn't go anywhere.

---

[11] Katie Sehl, "Organic Reach is in Decline—Here's What You Can Do About It," Hootsuite, August 24, 2021, https://blog.hootsuite.com/organic-reach-declining/.

We don't know a lot of people who go to other people's Facebook profiles and search their history for something they posted a year ago. We don't even know a lot of people who search for certain content on these platforms. You *can* search on Facebook or Instagram, but they're not built as search engines.

YOUTUBE:
NINE MILLION IMPRESSIONS—FOR FREE

In 2021, YouTube gave our real estate videos nine million impressions—for free. That means our videos were placed in front of nine million viewers in a one-year time frame. Think about that: It's a lot of people, even if some impressions were shown to the same viewer more than once. That's twice the total population of Dallas, our market.

That's why we believe YouTube is the most content creator-friendly platform out there. YouTube's whole goal is time spent on the platform watching videos. They want people to stay on their platform as long as possible, so they want to recommend videos that people will watch. That's the bottom line: YouTube wants to promote content people will watch. YouTube's interests, the viewer's interests, and the content creator's interests are aligned. Everyone wants the same thing.

YouTube only counts an impression if somebody sees your thumbnail on their screen for longer than one second. They don't count the people who are just sitting there scrolling and blow past your thumbnail. It only counts if they actually stop or open their home page, or log on, and you're one of the thumbnails on there long enough for them to take it in. That actually requires only a fraction of a second, so it gives them plenty of time to choose whether to watch your video. (That's why you always want to think carefully about your thumbnail, because it's always the first thing people are going to see. We'll cover that in detail in Part 2.)

YouTube is also a search engine. As long as you've optimized everything correctly and have done the search optimization on the backend (we'll cover that later too), then you're more likely to show up in the search results. When somebody searches and your videos pop up, that's organic; they're probably thinking, *Oh, this is the best fit for me. I'm going to watch this video.* They *choose* to watch it; you don't have to pay them to do it, and you don't have to pay YouTube either. And if they choose to watch a second, third, fourth, fifth, or sixth video, they're doing that on their own as well—and it's all at no cost to you.

What works for us can work for you too. And YouTube won't charge you to do it. In fact, better still, they'll pay you.

YOUTUBE'S REVENUE SHARE

YouTube has a revenue share program that gives us a slice of the ad revenue they generate from our videos. It's called the

Partner Program. In 2021 we made a little bit over $4,000 from that revenue share. We expect to double and even triple that revenue in 2022.

Now, generating revenue from ads shown with our videos isn't a goal of ours. We can make much more than that from a single house sale. Our only goal is to make the phone ring—period.

But as of this writing, no other platform that I'm aware of actually shares ad revenue with you. We didn't have to do anything special except agree to monetize our channel and get the amount of watch hours and subscribers that YouTube requires.

There's this too: YouTube is going to play ads with your video regardless of whether you agree to monetize your channel or not. If you turn off ads for your channel, that just means you're turning them off for the purposes of sharing in revenue. It doesn't mean YouTube's not going to run ads. In fact, they will run them at least at the beginning, in the middle, or the end of your videos. Monetizing your channel gives you some control over when ads appear as well as the type of ads YouTube shows.[12]

We decided that we might as well get paid for ads shown on the front and the backend of our videos. We turn off the ads in the middle because once somebody starts to watch a video, we want them to have an uninterrupted viewer experience. We're

---

[12] Alan Spicer, "Can YouTubers Control Which Ads Are Shown?", Alan Spicer.com, https://alanspicer.com/can-youtubers-control-which-ads-are-shown/.

not worried about making that extra ten dollars off that video, even though it could add up. We think if a viewer runs into ads too many times, it'll probably be a turnoff for them—even if they are an intentional viewer who wants to see what we have to share. We've had a number of people tell us that they binge-watch our videos, and that's much easier when you can run through the whole video once it's started. On the other hand, we also believe viewers are accustomed to seeing an ad at the beginning and end of a video. And remember, YouTube's going to display ads at the beginning and the end of a video regardless of whether you choose to monetize them—unless the viewer clicks on one of your playlists. A playlist is a loop that will feed all of your videos on that list in a row, without any ads or other suggested videos. Your playlist could be ten, twenty, or thirty videos long. YouTube will play the entire list without slipping ads or other suggested videos into the stream.

NINE MILLION IMPRESSIONS—AND GROWING

Again, YouTube gave us nine million impressions in 2021—for free. In fact, they paid us $4,000 in 2021 through their ad revenue share. If you'd paid a penny per impression on any other platforms we've discussed to get in front of nine million viewers, that would have cost you $90,000. Yes, you'd have generated a lot of leads, and you would have been left chasing them too.

It gets even better. In the first seven months of 2022, YouTube gave our videos more than ten million impressions. One video we published reached almost one million impressions on its own—in less than two weeks. Think about that. Can you think of another way to get in front of that many people that quickly? For free?

That's the power in pursuing a free versus paid marketing strategy using YouTube.

Free versus Paid Takeaway

A paid marketing strategy can buy you leads. A free marketing strategy using YouTube videos can bring you customers who've already decided they want to work with you—and even make you a little money through YouTube's ad revenue sharing.

CHAPTER 4

SEASONAL VERSUS EVERGREEN

When we say "seasonal," what comes to your mind? Maybe it's the lights and excitement of the Christmas season, the Halloween stores that open every October, or the Easter displays, decorations, and candy you see everywhere in the spring. As a small business owner, maybe you think about seasonal employees—adding an extra worker or two to handle the rush. But whatever the example that comes to your mind, seasonal means temporary. It comes and goes, lasting only for a short time.

How about "evergreen?" Well, an evergreen tree keeps its leaves all year long. That's where the term comes from. An evergreen tree is never leafless the way other trees are; it's always green. You could even say it's always relevant—and that's exactly how we think of seasonal versus evergreen content.

Which would you rather have? Evergreen content, right? Because it's relevant all year long, always there, always waiting to be found. And that's our point: when it comes to marketing, especially with video on YouTube, evergreen content provides the best opportunity to generate sustained business—because evergreen content can be searched, found, or recommended day after day, week after week, month after month, year after year. It's the best way to maximize the power of leverage through video.

SALES AT SCALE

Ultimately, evergreen video content is sales and communication at scale. Let's consider our business again. In real estate, you have conversations with clients every single day. If they come from out of town or even a different neighborhood, they might say, "Hey, could you take me around, show me the different neighborhoods, and explain why this one is nicer than that one, or why are homes more expensive over here versus over there?"

You're not likely to be reciting a script with all the stats and data on each neighborhood as you drive around. You're probably going to talk as you would with a friend. You might talk about a friend who lives there and what they think about it. Maybe you'll talk about the ways in which it's changed in the past ten or twenty years.

Here's the issue: That's a seasonal conversation. It lives and dies with that client on that day. Once the conversation is done, it's lost forever.

Now, imagine if you had a camera person with you in the car the whole time. Most people don't, of course, and it would be weird, unless you had a TV reality show—but the point is that they'd capture your conversation. That means it would live forever on whichever channel you decided to display it on.

The same concept applies in other businesses. We're talking about holding one-on-one conversations, customer by customer, every single day, versus making videos that last forever. If you're a plumber, you could be explaining why a faucet is leaking while standing in a puddle in someone's kitchen. If you're a financial advisor, you might be describing how a stock trade works to a new client on the phone. Those are seasonal conversations; make a video version, and it's evergreen. That video could reach 100, 1,000, 10,000, or even 100,000 people!

Evergreen content is everywhere. We don't watch a lot of TV, but whenever one of us clicks it on, we always seem to see the same episode of *Seinfeld, Friends,* or *Fixer Upper* that was on the last time we clicked on the TV. Has that ever happened to you? You're left thinking, how is this possible?

That's evergreen content. They're replaying it over and over and over again.

Now, what if it's content the customers you want are actively searching for? And if it's always there for them, always relevant, every day, night, weekend, month, or year?

"I CAN'T STAND DALLAS"

That's the beauty of an evergreen video on YouTube. It will be found over and over and over again. Not only do you get the initial views from when it's released, but you'll continue to capture views as long as that video lives on YouTube and is searchable.

Seasonal content is temporary; it's likely to die quickly. Evergreen content never stops working for you.

Here's an example of what we mean. We released a video titled "I Can't Stand Dallas" in May of 2021. By the end of the year, seven months later, it had more than 31,000 views. Pretty good, right? Well, in the next seven months, it got 40,000 additional views. More than a year after we made the video, it was still *gaining* momentum. YouTube was still promoting it through its "Suggested" and "Browse" features. (More on those a bit later.)

Why? Because it's evergreen. In the video, we talked about the things we don't like about Dallas. Those things were relevant to people moving to Dallas last year, this year—and they'll be relevant next year too. So it's still getting views. It's still getting traction. YouTube still sees it as relevant and is still pushing it out.

But it's also backed up by search. Every time someone searches the negatives about Dallas, it will likely pop up as well—even if YouTube stops promoting it. (More on that in a moment too.)

SEASONAL SHORTCOMINGS

Let's stay in the real estate space and compare that success to seasonal video. We see a lot of agents filming market reports: the latest figures on prices, home sales, and mortgage rates. And let's face it: a market report is as good as dead by the next week, the next month, or maybe, at best, the next two months. Unless you're a real estate historian, a market report from May of 2021 doesn't really serve much purpose. People just won't find it relevant. They'll jump off the video very quickly—and that triggers YouTube to say, "Okay, not a lot of people are interested in this video. Therefore, we're not going to promote it to more people because they're not sticking around to watch it." It won't be backed by search either, because who is going to search "May 2021 Dallas market update" after May 2021?

We see a lot of open house videos too. If you're saying, "Hey, I'm here at my open house at 123 Main Street," that's very specific. You're talking about a particular time and place. That's seasonal content. What's someone who finds it six months later going to say? "That's not relevant anymore. I'm going to jump off." The same thing goes for listing videos. They don't typically do well on

YouTube—unless they're in the multimillion-dollar range. A real estate agent who's doing a listing video, selfie-style, on a $500,000 house usually doesn't get a lot of traction on YouTube. In our opinion, all $500,000 homes look the same, so it's not necessarily interesting to many viewers. That said, we have found strategies to make listing videos evergreen. You can start out by walking down the street in the neighborhood instead of inside the house, or standing at an intersection outside a popular restaurant—broadening what you're presenting, giving a feel for what that money buys in that neighborhood beyond the house itself.

Creating content that is evergreen means the subject remains relevant and the information does too. When people find it, they'll see value in the content. It's a strategy that works over time, and that's primarily because of search.

THE POWER OF SEARCH

There are YouTube experts we respect who believe first and foremost in Suggested and Browse—categories that YouTube uses to point users toward videos that are finding an audience. Suggested videos appear alongside or after other videos; Browse videos appear on a user's homepage or in their feed.

That will give you a lot of views, especially on the front end. But as soon as YouTube decides to stop displaying it, those views will start to wind down.

That's why we put our emphasis on search. As long as the topics of your videos are searchable—with the right keywords in place and a title that's structured correctly—that video will remain relevant for the next two, three, four, and even five years. We'll often include the current year in a title to stress its relevance to someone who's searching for information, but if it's an evergreen video, you can always update the year in the title.

Yes, Suggested and Browse are powerful—very powerful. You want your videos to appear there. But you also don't want your video to die out once YouTube starts pulling back. That's why we structure things around search and have from the beginning.

WATER IN THE DESERT

You can think of YouTube as a desert, because it is vast. There were 800 million videos on YouTube in 2022.[13] Many of them were posted by people who think, *Oh, I'm going to upload my one video, and I'm going to go viral.* But the reality is that they're just throwing a grain of sand out there in the desert along with everyone else.

---

[13] Jason Wise, "How Many Videos Are on YouTube in 2022?", EarthWeb, updated July 22, 2022, https://earthweb.com/how-many-videos-are-on-youtube/.

Now, as of 2022, YouTube has 2.6 *billion* active monthly users.[14] They're wandering the desert, and they're thirsty.

As a content creator, you could have fifty gallons of water to offer. And you could just sit in one place, waiting for someone thirsty to wander by. You'll catch some stragglers coming over the sand dunes. "Oh my!" they'll say. "There's a guy with fifty gallons of water! I'm going to go over there and drink some."

But what if you're in the desert with that water, and you have the GPS coordinates of a little colony of people who are stuck under a palm tree, dying of thirst? What if you brought your water to them? Will they drink it? Absolutely. And guess what? They'll probably follow you wherever you go.

That's how we think of search-based videos on YouTube. First, you have to figure out what the people you're trying to reach are searching for. And then YouTube just puts the content in front of them.

That's how we started out. In the beginning, we didn't make videos simply because we wanted to make them. We made content on topics that were already being searched, and that helped us get found sooner rather than later. We optimized for the YouTube algorithm. (We'll explain how to do this in Chapter 12.) As we developed our audience and came to know them,

---

[14] GMI Blogger, "YouTube User Statistics 2022," June 28, 2022, https://www.globalmediainsight.com/blog/youtube-users-statistics/.

talking with them, selling them homes, and working with their families, we began to customize our videos around the questions they asked us. We optimized for our audience.

And what did both phases have in common? The content was evergreen and search-based.

We're not saying that you should never create seasonal content. In the real estate context, you can do a market report—especially if it's just a small part of the video rather than the entire video. If there's information on the front or backend that stays relevant, the video will stay relevant too.

"DOES IT SNOW IN TEXAS?"

Here's one form of seasonal content that works: videos that will come to life again when the next season comes around. We think of that as semi-seasonal content.

Here's an example. We get asked a lot if it snows in Dallas. Well, one day in February of 2021, we got what people call "The Texas Winter Storm of 2021." The amount of snow in Dallas was unprecedented. Instead of melting the next day, as it usually does, it dumped on us, and everything froze. It was there for a week. I went out and made a video, wearing a knit cap, gloves, and a winter jacket to show people the answer: Yes, we get snow in Texas. We called the video "Does It Snow in Texas?"—a search-friendly title, the way people would type it in a search bar—and even offered three winter survival tips for Texans.

We were utilizing what the book *YouTube Secrets*, co-authored by our friends Sean Cannell and Benji Travis, calls the tent pole strategy. Whenever you have a major event like the great winter storm, there's going to be a spike in search traffic, reflecting the spike in interest. If you can create content around that, you'll capture the spike, and that's great. Of course, you'll see a significant drop off from there.

In this case, as we just discussed, we added the winter survival tips to give the video relevance beyond February of 2021. We talked a bit about the neighborhood where we filmed it and the surrounding area as well, giving it one more search term that might bring viewers in.

Is that video relevant in July? No. But next winter, and for all the winters after that, it will be.

What's relevant in July? We get questions from clients all the time: "What happens in summer? You guys don't have beaches. You don't have mountains. So what do you do for fun?"

It's as if they think we just sit around and bake like a cookie on the side of the road.

We answered those questions with a video titled "Lake Living in Dallas Texas." There are five lakes within fifteen to twenty minutes of Dallas. You can go to any one of them, do some waterskiing, cliff jumping, or wake surfing. Here in Dallas in the summer, you grow up on the lake. (And guess what? There are no sharks in our lakes either. You can have your fun day at the beach in Florida or Hawaii. We'll stay safe here in our lakes.)

What makes this a semi-seasonal video? Well, it will rise again in search, every summer. So that's the key question to ask: Will it live again?

That said, it's not going to kill your channel if you make a seasonal video. You can make any video you want. But if you want it to work for you all day, every day, you need to make an evergreen video.

Seasonal versus Evergreen Takeaway

Seasonal content is temporary. It dies quickly. Evergreen content provides the best opportunity to generate business—because it's relevant day after day, week after week, month after month, year after year.

CHAPTER 5

SELFISH VERSUS SERVICE

So much of the marketing we're exposed to every day is selfish: it's all about the advertiser. But we've found sharing service-based content through videos on YouTube provides a much greater opportunity to attract business. Why? If you stop and think about it, unless you're a celebrity, no one is searching for you. What they're searching for is an answer to their questions, and that's what service-based content is all about.

People don't default to selfish-based advertising because they're intentionally selfish. It's because that's what most businesses do. They market themselves. It's been the way things are done forever.

LIMITS OF SELFISH-BASED MARKETING

Think about the forms selfish-based marketing takes: postcards, business cards, billboards, even magazine ads. How much can you say on any of those? Not much more than "Levi Lascsak, real estate agent, call today to buy, sell, or invest." Or "Number One Highest Production Team in Dallas." It's very hard to convey a message that provides value on something as small and limited as a postcard.

Then there's networking when people are out meeting and greeting. What are they likely to say? "Hi, my name's Travis, and I'm a real estate agent. Are you thinking about buying or selling in the next two, three, four, five, six months?" Most of the people they're talking to already know several real estate agents, and half of them are family members! It's not impossible to generate business that way—but it's difficult.

As we've said, small businesses most often fail because they're unable to generate leads effectively, given their tight budgets. Remember, in real estate, most agents come into the business with less than $5,000 to their name. That's a very limited budget, and even if an agent puts every dollar they've got into postcards or magazine ads, it doesn't go very far. It definitely won't get you a billboard—unless it's in an area of town where you may not even want to work. You could buy a ton of Facebook ads and generate a lot of leads—but you've still got to convert them. And that's an interruption platform, as we've discussed: people aren't typically going there to find a real estate agent or a car salesperson. Even if they are looking around, they may not be actively in the market for twelve, eighteen, even thirty-six months.

SELFISH-BASED MARKETING
ON YOUTUBE

We've even seen a lot of self-based marketing on YouTube. The first thing many people do is name their channel after themselves. One of the first things we realized when we researched YouTube was that "Levi Lascsak" was not a search term people were going to use. Nobody's out there searching "Travis Plumb," much as we'd like to think they are.

And what's the first video people often post? An introductory video. "My name's Levi Lascsak. I'm a real estate agent in Dallas, Texas. If you wanna buy, sell, or invest, I've been in real estate for fifteen years. I've done this and done that, and I can help you do whatever you need to do." Everybody typically has a video like that. It's often the first video they put on their channel—and you know what? It doesn't normally get a lot of traction. And that's no surprise. What gives them the right to ask someone for business when a person doesn't even know them?

We often see the same problem with the titles of listing videos. Nobody is specifically searching for "123 Main Street, Dallas,

Texas." That's a selfish-based video title. It's about trying to sell a house, not answering questions someone might have about moving to Dallas.

Here's the issue: The people making the videos are thinking about the information they want to get out there instead of what their customers are actually searching for. They're thinking it's all about selling themselves instead of providing value to people searching for answers to their questions and fulfilling their own needs.

A selfish-based mentality makes those channels and videos extremely difficult to find. And when people do find them, they feel like they are being sold. No one likes that. Our friend Ryan Serhant may be one of the most prominent real estate agents in the world, thanks to his YouTube channel, books, and Bravo television series, and here's how he puts it, "People hate being sold, but they love shopping with friends."

Remember, when we got started, nobody was searching for "Levi and Travis." But millions of people search "Dallas Texas" every month. There were hundreds of thousands of searches for individual suburbs and neighborhoods. You'll find the same dynamic no matter what business you're in. People probably aren't searching for you; they're more likely to be searching for answers.

SERVICE-BASED CONTENT
IN SMALL MARKETS

You may be in a smaller market than Dallas, and that's okay. Service-based marketing can work for you too.

If you're the first in your area to use YouTube marketing, guess what? You've got the best chance to be found. Even in smaller areas, you might be surprised by how many people are out there searching for answers to their questions.

You don't have to generate the volume of searches or the amount of business that we're doing here in Dallas to be successful. A smaller market will generate smaller volume. You have to ask yourself if two, three, or four transactions a month would change your business. Most of the time for most of the people we talk to, that answer is "absolutely, yes."

Consistency matters. You have to post videos. But even inconsistent posting can yield results if you're first to market. We've been working with a small-market real estate agent named Chris Owens, who lives in Northwest Georgia. Chris had no sales or real estate experience; he came from the nursing field. But when he heard about what we were doing, he thought it would be a great way for him to break into real estate too. Northwest Georgia is far from the largest real estate market in the country. It's very rural and not densely populated. But he started as we did, with YouTube videos about his area. Even though he had to drive thirty minutes between towns, he still provided value to people who were considering moving to that area. He heard from several clients, and he closed several deals. He's not working at the volume we are, but it was enough for him to provide for his family. Then he went two months without posting—which we do not recommend. But he's still closing deals. One buyer recently told Chris that the main reason they'd chosen him over the other agent in the area was that he had videos out there. The other agent didn't.

That gave Chris the advantage for the same reason videos bring people to us: They've come to know and trust us before we've even talked. The videos allow them to go shopping *with* us, rather than putting us or Chris in the position of trying to sell them something.

BE YOURSELF

It's very difficult to develop relationships with people through traditional, selfish-based marketing. Certainly some forms of traditional marketing have improved in this respect. Postcards have gotten very creative with QR codes people can scan and various calls to action. But oftentimes traditional marketing still comes down to hitting people over the head again and again and again. Our good friend, Michael Reese, co-author of *Digital President*, who relied on postcard marketing during his production years, told us that one customer finally called him and said, "I could wallpaper my whole house with your postcards." It was effective; he finally called. But it cost Michael thousands of dollars in postcards before he saw that return.

We believe it's through video that people can best get to know you and what you offer, beneath the surface level. That's why, with service-based video content, you have to be yourself. Don't be a character.

Of course, there are a lot of YouTubers out there who are characters, but they'll probably never meet their audience. If they're playing a character on YouTube, that's okay.

In real estate, the goal is to meet our audience. We're going to show them homes, spend time with them, and work with them to find the right home at the best price. The same dynamic is true in many businesses—so you want to be who you are.

That's especially important if you are self-conscious about being on video, as many people are. Just be yourself, and let people see you for exactly who you are. If you are a purple-haired real estate agent, guess what? Whoever calls you already knows they're going to be working with the purple-haired real estate agent.

We've found that people with English as a second language can be especially concerned about this. They're often anxious about meeting a client or speaking to someone for the first time. But if you make videos, the people who call you are going to know exactly what you sound like. They're only calling because they've seen the value you offer through your videos and they want your help. They want to do business with you. Your accent is irrelevant. We believe service-based videos can give you the best opportunity to capture the English-language market as well as the market of those who speak your native language.

It all comes down to the difference between selfish versus service-based marketing. We always try to think about what our viewer, our audience, our client is searching for, wherever they're at, and providing the information that will be most helpful to them. There's no better way to start a relationship.

BRINGING GRATEFUL CUSTOMERS TO YOU

Here's the difference that service-based video marketing can make.

Travis worked in car sales after leaving the service. That's a hard business. The challenge is getting clients, and you can end up in what feels like a fistfight over a $200 commission. The same goes for a lot of sales jobs.

But service-based YouTube videos capture people in the research phase. That's what we love about it most. They may not even have decided to hire a real estate agent when they start consuming your videos. But as they watch those videos, they develop a sense of relationship. And once they reach out, it's game over. They've already decided that they want to work with you. They have even narrowed their search because of your videos. They already know they want to be in Frisco or Prosper, Texas. They're dialed in. It saves time for everyone involved and makes the whole process easier.

That didn't happen very often for Travis in car sales. He felt like he was fighting tooth and nail for clients, and he didn't like it. Why do car salesmen have a bad rep? You go into a dealership with reluctance, because you already have the perception that someone's going to sell you something you don't want at a price that's higher than you want to pay. But if that car salesperson was making informational videos about the cars on their lot, explaining what they offer, what they don't, and why they're priced as they are—giving you all that information and value up front, maybe adding "Mention this video and I'll give you a discount"—then you have a friend. You know they are going to take care of you because of the content you've already watched.

These days the people who approach Travis are grateful, not fearful, and it's because of the information we've already provided them. That's why we're closing deals so much more quickly than is typically the case.

What works in our business will work in others. Who wouldn't want to bring more grateful customers to their door? People appreciate the value they see in service-based video marketing. It's good for them, and that's good for business too.

Selfish versus Service Takeaway

Traditional marketing is selfish; it's about selling yourself. Service-based video marketing that provides answers people are searching for delivers real value that will bring grateful customers to you.

CHAPTER 6

SHORT FORM VERSUS LONG FORM

It's often said that people have a shorter attention span than a goldfish. We're not sure how you'd actually measure a goldfish's attention span, and unless you're trying to market your business to goldfish, it doesn't really matter. But in 2015, researchers reported that the average human attention span is only 8.25 seconds—and falling. It's 4.25 seconds less than it was in 2000.[15] What that basically means is that we really don't have attention spans at all, because how much can you really focus on in eight seconds?

---

[15] Steven Zauderer, "Average Human Attention Span By Age (Infographic)", Cross River Therapy, August 29, 2022, https://www.crossrivertherapy.com/average-human -attention-span.

As a result, a lot of business owners are moving toward short-form content. We see it all the time in the real estate space. They think that those short-attention-span figures suggest they should. Whether the sound is on or off, whether viewers are already moving on—people are on their phones consuming short-form content, so that's where businesses typically want to be. It's where the eyeballs are.

On the surface, it does make sense. And it can work; we know people who are generating good business with short-form content.

But think about scrolling through short-form platforms, such as Facebook, Instagram, and TikTok. How long do you actually stay on a post? Do you typically click on the *read more*, or just scroll onto the next picture without even pausing? (A content creator has only three seconds to hook someone's attention.[16]) When you're watching videos, is the sound on or off? (In public, most people watch with the sound off; on Facebook, the figure is 85 percent.[17]) Are you even looking to be hooked—or distracted?

Our experience has shown us that long-form content has a distinct advantage over short-form in generating conversions.

---

[16] Rich Meyer, "You have 3 seconds to gain attention online," New Media and Marketing, September 19, 2020, https://www.newmediaandmarketing.com/you-have-3-seconds-to-gain-attention-online/.

[17] Sahil Patel, "85 percent of Facebook video is watched without sound," Digiday, May 17, 2016, https://digiday.com/media/silent-world-facebook-video/.

That's because even in this day and age, people aren't *always* distracted. Not when they're searching for answers. Why? It all goes back to their intentions—and the opportunity to build a relationship that long-form content presents.

WHAT OUR NUMBERS SHOW

Our analytics bear this out. We've shared them before: 53 percent of our traffic comes from TV, computer, and tablet. What do all three have in common? They're research devices. Up to 70 percent of all web traffic comes from mobile devices; on Facebook, it's 95 percent.[18] But for us, that figure is only 47 percent.

Our viewers don't just come and go either. On TV, which accounted for 28 percent of our traffic in 2021, the watch-time duration on average was nine minutes and thirty-six seconds. For the record, that's seventy-two times longer than the average human attention span of eight seconds!

We've heard statistics suggesting that it takes six minutes of online video consumption for somebody to build a relationship with you. If you're doing only short-form content and none of your videos are longer than sixty seconds, that suggests someone would have to see at least six videos to begin feeling a connection.

---

[18] Aleksandar S., "What Percentage of Internet Traffic Is Mobile in 2022?", TechJury, Updated June 8, 2022, https://techjury.net/blog/what-percentage-of-internet-traffic-is-mobile/.

If you're doing thirty-second videos, they'd need to see twelve videos. As we've discussed, that's assuming they're actively in the market for whatever it is you're offering; otherwise, you're just interrupting them when they're trying to do something else.

Why are we seeing nine-and-a-half-minute watch times? It's not because we're that charismatic or make amazing videos. It's because our viewers are researching their next move—and when people are researching, they give it their full attention. They really are locked in. Their attention span is at its greatest. When you know their intention, you will have their attention.

Moving is one of the top five stressors in people's lives, right behind death and divorce. It's ahead of a major illness or injury and losing your job.[19] It's a family decision with life-changing effects for everyone involved. The people who come to us are often from outside the area. They can't just drive around to check things out, but they want to explore the area before they make a move here. So they're sitting down, digging in, and watching our content.

But that doesn't mean long-form videos won't work for plumbers, financial advisors, and other businesses too. According to Microsoft research, 72 percent of searchers consider the results they find trustworthy, the highest of any digital channel.

---

[19] "The Top 5 Most Stressful Life Events and How to Handle Them," University Hospitals, July 3, 2015, https://www.uhhospitals.org/Healthy-at-UH/articles/2015/07/the-top-5-most-stressful-life-events.

YouTube is the second-most used search engine, behind only Google; people are going on there to get their questions answered. (Think about it: Where would you go to learn how to change a bicycle tire? What a great place for your local bike shop to be!) And more and more people are moving toward video—where they can see a demo—before making a purchase.[20] That's why these days, you'll see videos when you click on many products on Amazon.

FROM LONG FORM TO SHORT FORM

We don't look at TikTok, Facebook, or Instagram as our primary marketing outlets, but we do want to be represented there—if only to drive users to our YouTube channel. And that brings us to another advantage of long-form content: It's much easier to make ten, one-minute videos out of a single ten-minute video than it is to assemble ten, short-form videos into a long-form video. What works in one direction—repurposing content from long form to short—just doesn't work going the other way. And that allows us to have the presence we want on the other platforms while minimizing the time that's required to do it. (It's also worth noting that YouTube recently made posting short videos

---

[20] "135 Video Marketing Statistics You Can't Ignore in 2022," Invideo, March 4, 2021, https://invideo.io/blog/video-marketing-statistics/.

more beneficial, at least from our point of view. We'll cover that change in Chapter 14.)

An editor can identify the start and end points in a long-form video and extract nuggets in clips lasting fifteen, thirty, forty-five, and all the way up to sixty seconds. It's a great way to leverage your time. Think about it: you could extract forty, fifteen-second clips out of a single, ten-minute video. That's an entire month's worth of content for the other platforms.

That said, it's always best to upload content that's specifically designed for the platform where you're posting it. We recognize that. We're not expecting to generate a huge following or a lot of business from Facebook, TikTok, and Instagram. Those aren't our primary goals, but we do want the presence.

We only post our long-form videos on YouTube; it's where we find viewers with intention. If we did share one on another platform, and someone clicked on it, we'd get the view count—but they wouldn't be signed in. That means YouTube wouldn't know who they were, so it couldn't feed them more of our videos the next time they visited YouTube. Their sound will be off by default, and if someone on a short-form platform clicked through to a ten-minute video, they'd say "I don't have time for that" and move on. It's not the best fit for our content. I think of this in terms of platform psychology. If someone who is trying to kill time is just scrolling through silly, entertaining, and fun videos, they are likely not in the mood to watch a long-form video, especially about moving. That is why we don't recommend sharing your YouTube videos on all of the other social platforms.

We want people when they're sitting down and ready to learn, and we want to make it as easy as possible for YouTube to find that audience for us. That means we want them when they're signed in and searching on Google or YouTube. If they're on Google, they're probably signed in on their Chrome browser or on a Google account, so YouTube knows who they are. We only list our YouTube channel link on our Google business page; that's important.

Otherwise, we simply say, "Search us on YouTube to find more."

SHOPPING WITH FRIENDS

Have you ever watched a TV show because your partner made you do it? After the first episode, you might be thinking to yourself, *I can't stand this show. I'll never watch it again.* But the next week, there's your partner watching it again—so you sit down, hang out, and catch a bit of it. By the third or the fourth episode, you're dialed in. You're starting to enjoy it. You're starting to like some characters, maybe hate some others—but you're starting to build relationships. The next thing you know, you can't wait for the next season. We know; it's happened to us.

That's why most people love movie stars. They see them on-screen; they hear their voice; they develop a relationship with them. That's also why *Friends* had a cast of six friends, all with different personalities. If you didn't like Joey, you might relate to Ross, and that might be enough to keep you watching the show. You and your real friends begin to see yourselves in the characters: you're like Ross, I'm like Joey, she's like Rachel.

Remember: people like shopping with friends—and shopping with friends takes time. When was the last time you bought something based on sixty seconds of learning? Whether you are selling a car, explaining a retirement account, or selling a house, it takes much longer than sixty seconds in real life. Long-form video is simply sales at scale. You are recording your sales process and publishing it to far more people than you could ever talk to in a day.

Long-form content allows potential clients to spend extended time with you. They see you at different stages of the sales process, dressed in different ways on different days. They get to know you through your long-form videos. They come away with a sense of what it's like to work with you over a day, week, or month. That really matters when you've got a long sales cycle, as we do in real estate. Still, as we've said, our average time from contact to contract is forty-seven days, far faster than the norm—because our clients don't approach us until they are in the buying process, ready to make a decision. They've already come to think of us as friends who are there to help them.

There's no better position for a business to be in—and we believe long-form content is the best opportunity for any business to get there. Long-form content comes with an added bonus: it can be chopped up to make short-form content too.

Short Form versus Long Form Takeaway

Short-form videos may seem like the best way to match people's shrinking attention spans. But we've found that long-form videos offer the best way to build relationships that lead to business. You can also repurpose long-form videos for short-form platforms and get exposure there too.

CHAPTER 7

LOCAL VERSUS GLOBAL REACH

One decision any business owner has to make is the size of the market they want to reach. Maybe it's a very small, local market. If that's the case, YouTube marketing can help you farm it like no one else. We met a real estate agent at a conference whose "farm area" is only 800 homes—but he owns 90 percent of the market. Nine out of every ten homes that sell in that area go through him and his team. That's significant.

But what if you want to attract business from outside your local area? What if your market is bigger—regional, national, even global—and your ambitions are too? Our success in Dallas real estate shows that YouTube marketing can reach anyone anywhere who's searching for the answers you provide. That's because YouTube has global reach. And these searchers can find you anytime they're looking, 24/7/365. We know, because we've seen it in our relocation business—from people from all over the world who are looking to move to Dallas.

These are amazing clients to work with. They're extremely motivated. They're intentional, not casual, so they're in decision-making mode. Fortunately for us, they're likely to be selling more expensive homes in other places. So they're coming with cash; they have a timeline; and they're likely to stick with it. Sometimes circumstances pop up that stop them from moving to Dallas, but not very often. They don't know any other realtors in Dallas, but because of our videos, they feel like they know us even before they reach out—and they know what they want too.

We love hearing from people looking to relocate, which we often do. We have YouTube to thank for the opportunity. How else would they ever find us, over any other realtor in Dallas? It goes beyond Texas or elsewhere in the country. We've heard from people in Belgium, Australia, Canada, Japan, and other countries too. Our Belgian client was an American who'd been living overseas for six years. Her email began with "I've been watching your videos"—and that's almost always how it begins. For clients like these, ultimately, we don't have any competition. They've decided they want to work with us before we even hear from them. As we've said before, that makes the conversion process much shorter than the norm.

We once helped a client find a house in Plano, outside Dallas, and when he moved in, he found that both of his next-door neighbors were real estate agents. In 2020, there were nearly 12,000 active real estate agents in Dallas;[21] we told him that he could throw a rock and find one. "It's funny," he told us after his move. "You really *can* throw a rock and hit a real estate agent in this market." But he didn't have to throw a rock. He found us through YouTube.

If you're in real estate and near a military base—or any business with a particular interest in serving the military—you should absolutely be on YouTube. Travis and I are both combat veterans, so we know how it goes in the military. When the military says that you have to move, you have to move. The service usually gives you about a sixty-day timeline, if that—and it's likely to be a place that you've never been before. A soldier could be in South Korea, Japan, Germany—any of the international duty stations—and suddenly they learn that their next assignment is going to be Fort Campbell, Kentucky. They could live on-base, but many soldiers prefer a home off-base, and if they've got a family, they want to know where they'll be living before they get there. They have no idea where to look, or who's a good plumber, electrician, car dealer—you name it, all the things you need to know to thrive

---

[21] "Top Dallas Real Estate Agents," *U.S. News & World Report*, https://realestate.usnews.com/agents/texas/dallas/.

in a new community. YouTube is a search engine; they're likely to look there. So why wouldn't you want to be there too?

IT'S ALWAYS DAYTIME SOMEWHERE

When it's 3:00 a.m. in Dallas, it's 9:00 a.m. in London. While we're sleeping, someone in London may be watching our videos. Someone in Okinawa could be too; 3:00 a.m. in Dallas is 5:00 p.m. there. For someone at their desk In New Delhi, it's 1:30 p.m. For an early riser in Florida, it's 4:00 a.m.; for a night owl in Sacramento, it's 1:00 a.m.

And on a given day, any one of them could be thinking of moving to Dallas and looking at our videos. Our analytics make this clear. Here are a couple numbers from one recent, forty-eight-hour stretch:

- ▶ 2:00 a.m.: 69 views
- ▶ 3:00 a.m.: 70 views
- ▶ 4:00 a.m.: 72 views

That may not seem like a lot. But if you're in real estate, like us, when's the last time that you cold-called sixty-nine people at 2:00 a.m.? (We wouldn't recommend it.) When's the last time you knocked on the doors of seventy homes at 3:00 a.m.? (We wouldn't recommend that either.) When's the last time you mailed out a round of marketing postcards at 4:00 in the morning? (It's easier to wait until the post office opens.)

YouTube videos allow you to "meet" people on their research time, whenever it is that they're looking for information. Remember, it's intentional-based marketing. No matter what the hour, they're coming to you. You're not interrupting their dinner, their work, or whatever else they'd rather be doing than talking to you. The most common form of rejection isn't a no. It's "This is not a good time for me." That's the everyday reality most people in sales face, most of the time, and it's a big part of why salespeople often don't last.

STANDING OUT

Imagine if we'd try to launch our real estate business by doing the same things that thousands of other active agents in Dallas were already doing—many of them were well-established and widely known. How far would we have gotten by sending out postcards, advertising on Facebook, or calling FSBOs and Expireds? And how quickly would we have gotten anywhere?

Not very far and not very fast.

Open up any of the local magazines in Dallas—some of them down to the neighborhood level, and focused on real estate—and count the number of ads from real estate agents. The last time we did that, 135 different agents had ads in one magazine, all trying to farm that single area. And yet we'll hear agents say, "Well, I think YouTube is saturated, because I saw one agent making videos." That just shows the power of the herd mentality—and the cost of running with that herd is high, because those ads can be expensive.

We once ran an experiment, advertising in a hyper-local magazine that goes to 150,000 doors. It wasn't a general interest magazine; it was targeted to real estate. It seemed like a great test. A full-page ad cost $3,000 a month—and that was inside, where our ad was placed: next to the letters to the editor. The back cover cost $5,000 or $6,000. We structured the ad so we could track the calls and visits to our website that it generated—and it was nowhere close to YouTube. People who call tell us they love our videos all the time; no one who got that magazine called us to say, "I just loved your magazine ad. That was amazing!" And why would they? If they actually were in the market when they picked up the magazine, rather than just passing the time by looking at house pictures and prices, they'd be suffering from decision fatigue as they turned the pages, trying to choose an agent, sitting there thinking, *Eenie meenie minie mo, who should I call?*

Paying for social media exposure can be a frustrating mystery too. It's difficult to get through to people, and then to build a rapport. You need to post multiple times a day; that's time consuming. So is responding to the leads you get, because you will get leads; converting them is the challenging part. It's interruption marketing, so you need to retarget too—segmenting your responses, and that means you may need the help of an ad agency. It gets expensive, especially when you pause to consider your Return On Investment (ROI).

We've never heard of a real estate agent who has proactively run ads in another country, cold-called there, or sent out mailers. Why would you ever spend money to do that? The people you reach may not even speak English. But anyone who can speak English can find our channel, and if they're looking to move to Dallas, YouTube will lead them to us.

YouTube is free. It creates relationships for you. It's available to searchers anywhere, anytime, from the comfort of their home and on their timetable. From the content creator's side, learning how to use YouTube effectively isn't rocket science. In all these ways, YouTube flattens the curve, and that's what makes it great.

Local versus Global Takeaway

If you're looking to farm a local market, YouTube can help you own it. And if your market and your ambitions are bigger, YouTube can bring you customers searching for the answers you offer anywhere, anytime—even from around the globe.

CHAPTER 8

TAKE TIME VERSUS MAKE TIME (AND BEYOND)

The number one reason small business owners, especially real estate agents, tell us that they don't get started on YouTube is because they don't have the time to do it. And we usually say, "If you don't have time to make videos for YouTube, that's exactly why you *should* make videos for YouTube. Clearly their time is not leveraged effectively, and that's what this is all about—leverage.

As we've said, all video is communication and sales at scale. Therefore, whenever you make a video, it's giving you the opportunity to make time. We'll say it again: it doesn't take you time; it *makes* you time. Better still, it can *compound* your time—and that's the path to dominating your market and ultimately liberating you.

We believe video is the true four-hour workweek. If you've read the book, *The 4-Hour Workweek* by Tim Ferriss, you know its central concept: leveraging other people and processes so that you just have to check in an hour a day, four days a week, to make sure that everything is functioning properly.

We know it is possible, although we haven't gotten there yet with our business. But making videos? That *is* a four-hour workweek. In fact, we spend less than four hours a week making videos—maybe even less than two hours a week. Those videos return so much value that it's the best investment of our time.

THE TRUE TIME TAKERS

In our opinion, it's the most popular alternatives to YouTube—Instagram, Facebook, and Tiktok—that take too much time. That's because succeeding on those platforms requires multiple posts per day.

If you listen to any Instagram marketer in 2022, they will tell you that you need to post two reels and ten stories every single day. And you've got to do that seven days a week if you want to stay relevant on the platform and grow. On top of that, you've got to add the right hashtags to every one of those posts.

That is very labor intensive—especially since those stories disappear. They only have a shelf life of twenty-four hours. Reels typically get most of their views within twenty-four to forty-eight hours as well. That's why they want you posting two reels per day.

TikTok takes time too. Social media guru Gary Vaynerchuk said that if you want to be relevant on TikTok in 2023, you need to post four TikToks per day. Think about that: not only do you have to make that content, but you've got to edit your own stuff, as people typically do, and you've got to post it too. On top of that, you've got to come up with something creative that fits within their sixty-second window. That's hard to do. Yes, they're shorter videos, but making them still interrupts your day. If you're batch recording, that's still four videos per day. Multiply that out, and you're talking 120 videos to plan and create every month.

Posting on Facebook has become a complete waste of time, in our opinion. The average reach of an organic post is only about 5 percent of your audience these days.[22] It is strictly a pay-to-play platform. Facebook wants you to pay to push your post out to even the people you know, those who have volunteered to be your followers. That means Facebook isn't just taking your time; it's taking your money too.

THE YOUTUBE SWEET SPOT

The sweet spot for YouTube long-form videos is one to three times per week. YouTube actually promotes the fact that they

---

[22] Katie Sehl, "Organic Reach is in Decline—Here's What You Can Do About It," Hootsuite, August 24, 2021, https://blog.hootsuite.com/organic-reach-declining/.

want your videos to breathe. Clearly, there are channels that post every day and they do well. That's okay for them. You've got to find your own rhythm and decide what works best for you. One to three videos a week is where most creators usually start.

When we got started in Dallas, there were a few real estate agents already creating YouTube videos—but they were only publishing one video per week. We realized that if we wanted to catch and possibly pass them, we'd need to outwork and out-publish them. We chose to be aggressive about posting because, after all, they were two or three years ahead of us.

Since the other agents were posting only one video a week, we posted three, thereby tripling their efforts. Within eighteen months, we had become the Number One real estate channel in Dallas. We had passed the channels we looked up to as benchmarks based on our goals, with more subscribers and views.

MAKING TIME

Our YouTube analytics show that YouTube does not take us time. It actually *makes* us time. If it takes us thirty minutes to make one video in totality, as soon as that video is watched for thirty-one minutes, we've got a one-minute profit on our time. That makes the investment of time well worth it. Even if that video were to die off immediately after that, we'd still have made a profit of one minute.

But in fact, our returns are much better. Our "I Can't Stand Dallas" video is one of our most popular. It's a twenty-eight-minute video, and we made it together. We filmed it in one take—so it literally took us twenty-eight minutes to make that video.

It has been watched for well over 9,000 hours.

Let's calculate the profit on that investment. If we take 9,000 hours and subtract thirty minutes, we've got a time profit of 8,999.5 hours. Divide that by twenty-four hours in a day, and it's the equivalent of 374 days. So that video has delivered more than one year of profit in prospecting for our thirty-minute investment. Even better, it is still getting more and more views every day!

In addition, it's reached more than 70,000 viewers. We could never make that many phone calls or knock on that many doors. It would take us months to send out 70,000 postcards, and it would cost us a fortune to do it too.

Did that video take us time or make us time? The answer couldn't be more clear.

COMPOUNDING TIME

It gets even better. Not only do YouTube videos make us time, they compound our time. It's an exponential effect, and we believe it's the key to market domination and financial independence.

In 2021, our first year, the videos we posted on our YouTube channel generated 66,600 watch hours. That's equivalent to 7.6 years.

Think about that. Our channel prospected 7.6 years in a one-year time frame. That's why we're able to generate the amount of business we do. We compounded the number of people we were able to get in front of.

Let's say our "competition" is able to make two hours of prospecting calls in one day, the old-school way. Our analytics show that in a single day, our channel has been watched for as many as 399.1 hours. That's equivalent to sixteen *days* of prospecting in that one day—as opposed to two *hours* of calling by the competition.

How is anyone doing it the old-school way ever going to catch us? If they're just starting out now, they're not going to. Some of our competitors have been doing it the old-school way for twenty years, and we respect that—it's the way they generate their business. But if you're old-school, what happens when you go on vacation? Or when you go to conferences? You're not making those calls or knocking on doors. You're not meeting people at big events or over coffee at Starbucks. However it is that you generate business, you're not prospecting in your down time if it's dependent on your effort.

Our record so far in one day is 1,514 watch hours. That is equivalent to 2.1 months. In July 2022, our channel was watched for 11,800 hours. That is equivalent to 1.34 years. In the first 1.5 years of our channel, it's been watched for 130,400 hours. That is equivalent to 14.88 years, or one and a half decades.

In terms of prospecting, our channel is turning days into months, months into years, and years into decades.

THE CASHFLOW QUADRANT

As a business owner, you're not only looking to get a return on your time, you're looking to compound your time. You may have heard of the book *Rich Dad, Poor Dad* co-authored by Robert T. Kiyosaki. He followed that bestseller with *Rich Dad's Cashflow Quadrant: A Guide to Financial Independence.* That book is about moving from the left side of that quadrant—where you're trading time for money, whether you're self-employed or working as an employee—to the right side, where you're a business owner or investor, freed from the constraints of trading time for money.

We didn't get a real estate license because we wanted to be employees. We didn't want to work for somebody else, and we didn't want to trade our time for money. But if you're simply self-employed (the S Quadrant), you're still on the left side of the cashflow quadrant. You're not leveraged. You're still trading time for money; you're just doing it for yourself instead of somebody else.

That's why real estate agents burn out. They stress out when they go on vacation, because they know they're not doing what they're supposed to be doing to build their business. It's hard to relax at the beach if you feel that you're falling further behind by the minute. Think about it this way: if you're in a relationship, making videos is the absolute best thing you can do. (This is not counseling, by the way.) That's because you can travel or take the weekends off or whatever it is you want to do—and enjoy yourself with your partner, because you know your videos are prospecting for you.

Now you're on the right side of the quadrant. In Kiyosaki's terms, you're not an Employee or Self-Employed any longer. You're a Business Owner.

In real estate, there are really only a few ways to achieve that. You can start a team, start a brokerage—or have something that is generating business for you twenty-four hours a day. Maybe you've seen the Warren Buffett quote: "If you don't find a way to make money while you sleep, you will work until you die." Here's our twist on it: "You'll never have a business until you can learn how to generate leads in your sleep."

If your lead generation is directly tied to your efforts, then you still have a job. Anytime you stop—the second you hang up that phone, the second you stop knocking on doors—your lead generation stops. You can't escape your job and become a business until you change that.

THE ULTIMATE STEP

The most coveted quadrant isn't Business Owner. It's Investor. Why is that? Because when you're an investor, that means your money makes you money. It's doing the work for you. That's where almost everybody wants to be.

Now: what's the first question you ask when you consider an investment? It's usually, "What's going to be the return?" You want to know how much an investment is going to give back, and how long it's going to take.

If time is our most valuable asset, why would you not ask yourself the same question whenever you're investing your time into something? Whether your time is going into social media, phone calls, door knocking, or any other type of lead generation, why wouldn't you ask, "What is going to be the return on my time?"

That's why we love YouTube. It doesn't take you time. It makes you time—and beyond that, it compounds your time. That's the story our backend analytics tell. Our bottom line tells the same story. We made more than $1 million in gross commissions in our first year, and we tripled the amount of business we did in 2021 in the first eight months of 2022. We did it through YouTube videos.

A SELLABLE ASSET

Here's one more very important factor in YouTube's compounding effect: a YouTube channel is a sellable asset. You can transfer ownership.

We built our channel with this in mind. We can show the analytics, which demonstrate its value. And we didn't name it Levi and Travis's Home Selling Team. That would make it much more difficult to sell our channel if we took ourselves out of it. Instead, we called it "Living in Dallas Texas." You can think of it as another dimension of Selfish versus Service-Based Content: it's not about promoting us; it's about serving the people who want to live in Dallas. We don't have to be present for the channel to work—so now it's a sellable asset.

Based on the business we generated in our first year, we could've sold the channel at the end of 2021 for about $3 million. That would have been nice if we wanted a $3 million buyout—but we knew it would generate far more for us in 2022. The value of the channel will rise right alongside the business it helps us generate.

We don't want to sell real estate until we're eighty—and we certainly don't want to be cold calling or door knocking when we're eighty either. We want to build a viable business that can still function and continue to grow after we step away from it.

That's the ultimate value in putting YouTube to work for your business too—and we don't believe you can do that as effectively with any other platform.

Take Time versus Make Time (and Beyond) Takeaway

Making YouTube videos doesn't take you time. It makes you time. Better still, it compounds your time—creating opportunities no other platform can match.

CHAPTER 9

ACTIVE VERSUS PASSIVE PROSPECTING

Travis and I both love sales—but we hate prospecting. Until we discovered the power of search-based YouTube marketing, we had both spent our entire working careers pursuing sales, all day, every day. That's the way a lot of businesses work. It's the entire reason for the industry of sales training, sales books, sales materials, and sales conferences. It's all focused on helping people become better at sales. Which is to say, better at what we call active prospecting.

How great would it be if you could sell without active prospecting?

We believe you can—with what we call passive prospecting. We've explained the basic principles of passive prospecting in the chapters that make up Part 1 of this book. This is the last of them: active versus passive prospecting. It's what everything else makes possible.

In Part 2, we'll get into the passive prospecting process: an introduction to how to go about building your business in the same way we built ours, using search-based YouTube marketing that brings customers to you instead of forcing you to chase them down.

But first, we want to illustrate the difference passive versus active prospecting can make using my story as an example. You can think of it as a before-and-after story: before passive prospecting—and after.

FROM THE HEALTH CLUB TO COSTCO

I started in sales twenty years ago in a health club, selling gym memberships with my good friend, Michael Reese. Ten to twelve hours a day, we made phone calls, trying to get five appointments for the next day. Once we got someone in the gym for a tour, we were likely to sell them a membership. But it literally took us ten hours of calls to get just five appointments.

I took a little hiatus—after serving in the Army, I was still in the National Guard, and I got deployed to Iraq. When I came home, I got into selling cell phones at Costco. Nobody goes to Costco intending to buy a cell phone, right? So I was always in pursuit, thinking of creative ways to interrupt people as they shopped for one hundred rolls of toilet paper, lawn chairs, or whatever else they needed long enough to get them to talk and even consider the possibility of upgrading or buying a cell phone. "Hey," I'd say, "can I pay for fifty dollars' worth of your groceries today?" The cell phones had a fifty dollar rebate, and that's how I'd get people to stop. But I might have to talk to 100 or 150 or even 200 people a day to get two or three to stop, talk, and buy a cell phone.

FROM PHARMACEUTICALS
TO PENSION PLANS

From cell phones, I got recruited into a pharmaceutical company. Now I was actively prospecting for doctors willing to prescribe the medications my company offered. Doctors expected these calls; it was a regular part of their business. But I still had to figure out when they were going to be in the office. I had to get past their gatekeepers. And if it was a popular doctor who prescribed a lot of medications, I had to get there thirty minutes early or I'd find eight other pharmaceutical sales reps in the waiting room. It was always a pursuit.

And then I had to try to educate a doctor. Think about that. I'd gone through a few weeks of training; the doctor had gone through years and years of schooling. And there I was, educating them on a medication. I had to develop relationships, build rapport, establish credibility. And they'd say, "Well, I can just read the literature, right?" I had to overcome a lot of barriers.

Then I started my own financial services business, and we ended up getting a contract with the Dallas Independent School District. I was working with teachers on retirement planning, and I had a captive audience of 25,000 employees—which was great. But what was I doing again? I was in pursuit. I had to market and reach out to teachers, making a hundred calls to get a few appointments, all in hopes of helping them with their retirement accounts. And here I was, a stranger meeting someone for the first time, in their free period, after they'd spent the day with the kids in their classrooms, having very intimate conversations about their finances in a very short time frame.

I was successful at every stage. I sold a lot of gym memberships and a lot of cell phones at Costco. I sold a lot of medications, and a lot of retirement plans to teachers. But in each of those businesses, I had to go after people on a constant basis. And I had to talk to a hundred people to try to get ten to actually have a conversation with me, hoping to get one or two deals in a day. That's what it boiled down to. And that's one of the big reasons why sales is a high turnover field.

A REJECTION-BASED BUSINESS

Active prospecting is hard. It's not easy to do. You have to have a lot of tenacity. You have to overcome objections. And you have to be able to take rejection, because sales is a rejection-based business.

If you're in sales, you'll hear motivational speakers and sales trainers tell you that every no gets you closer to a yes. You're told you have to get ten no's to get one yes—sometimes even more than that. It can be very painful. A lot of people don't like it. They prefer a path of less resistance, and for good reason. Who really enjoys rejection all day, everyday?

That's the challenge in active prospecting: it's difficult to do. Next we'll get back to my story.

FROM ACTIVE TO PASSIVE PROSPECTING

Along the way I got some experience in real estate. I was a part-time investor in one or two fix and flips per year, and I had seven rentals at one time. I still do Airbnb. And I had a lot of successful real estate agent friends—but I knew how hard they worked in the first few years to establish their brand, build credibility, and generate business. Why? Because that's typically how you're told to get started in real estate: through active prospecting. We've talked about the postcards, the door knocking, the cold calling before; a lot of agents are willing to do that because they have more time in the beginning than they do money.

After a lifetime in sales, I wasn't willing to do that in real estate. But I needed to do something different, because in 2020, the pandemic shut my financial services business down. I knew that if I was going to transition to something different, this was the time to do it.

And I realized that when I got out of selling gym memberships, cell phones, pharmaceuticals, or financial services, there was nothing there. When outside forces stopped me cold in my tracks, I didn't have anything to show for it. The moment I stopped working, the income stopped too. There was nothing left over.

Why was that? Because I was the focal point of my business. Everything was dependent on me. Maybe that's necessary in the beginning, when you have to save money and figure out how things work—but as soon as you can scale, by starting to add systems, processes, and people into the mix, that's what you need to focus on.

It was August of 2020. I decided things needed to change.

I began by asking myself questions. If I was going to get into real estate, how would I attract business? Was there a way to bring it to me, to get people to want to work with me? After all, I'd be competing with every real estate agent in Dallas, one of the biggest markets in the country for real estate, going up against established brands, brokerages, and people who have been in real estate for decades.

Was I going to walk in, send out some postcards, and attract some business? Not likely.

That's what got me thinking about social media. I began by investigating Facebook, Instagram, Tiktok—the standard go-to's. None of them sat well with me. They didn't fit my personality, and I didn't see a path to the kind of success I wanted.

YouTube was my last choice. As I dug in, I learned that it's not a social media platform. It's a search engine. That's when I understood its potential, because as a search engine, it could bring clients to me. All I had to do was find the answers they were already searching for and create content based on their needs.

Once I settled on YouTube, I developed a business plan. I had devoted two months—September and October—to my research. (I knew that if I treated YouTube like a hobby, it would pay me like a hobby. But if I treated it like a business, it could pay me like a business.) Then I began filming. That took me through November 2020.

On December 5, 2020, I released my first video. That month brought no sales, and no commissions. We gained forty-eight subscribers and got 1,900 views.

January 2021 brought us our first call—a $1 million-dollar home buyer—but no sales. We gained 348 subscribers and got 19,700 views.

February: no sales. But we gained 731 subscribers, got 49,000 views, and we topped 5,200 watch hours.

Seven months had passed since I'd chosen my new direction, and I had no sales to show for it. But the videos were out there prospecting for me, 24/7. I wasn't an overnight success—yet—but success was coming.

March brought no sales either—but we gained 1,300 subscribers, 92,300 views, and 9,300 watch hours. But I got my first deal under contract. Travis joined me, and he's a master closer. Two closed transactions followed in April, three in May, six in June—and the numbers kept growing. October and November brought eleven transactions each. In December—a year after launch—we closed eight deals. We added 7,800 subscribers, got 621,700 views, and 66,600 hours of watch time. In the last nine months of 2020, we closed sixty-four transactions leading to $1,007,000 in commissions.

We were on our way.

And neither of us had knocked on a single door, made a single cold call, or mailed out a single postcard. Every client had reached out to us, through phone, text, emails, and Zoom calls. It was 100 percent inbound, and on their terms and timeline.

That's passive prospecting—and that's what it can do for you and your business.

SCALING YOURSELF

Travis and I had each been selling for twenty years before making the transition from active to passive prospecting. The problem was that for every day during those twenty years we were selling to individuals, explaining the features and benefits of whatever it was we were selling. One to one, over and over. And when each day ended, so did our selling. When we turned off the lights and went home for the day, that was it. The next morning, we'd come in again and start over.

That's not scalable.

We've said it before and we'll say it again, because it's important: video is communication and sales at scale. Your videos allow you to sell yourself, and they do it over and over, whether you're working or not. Every video you make builds your success. Each one gives people who find your content more to watch—and that builds the rapport, credibility, and the relationship that leads to success.

Better still, your videos live forever. They'll never stop working for you.

That's scalable.

Today, we can travel. We can go to conferences. We can take time off. We've built an amazing team. When we're not working, everything's still running without us. Videos are still getting published. Homes are still being sold. Our team liberates us from devoting 10 percent of our effort to the ten things that always need to be done; now we're devoting 100 percent of our effort to the things that only we can do. That's going to generate the best return on our business.

The best thing of all: we're in a rejection-free business. (Well, aside from an occasional comment on one of our videos. Those can get interesting.) But our customers come to us, and they've already decided they want to work with us.

The videos are doing the hard work for us. And that's the power of passive prospecting.

Active versus Passive Prospecting Takeaway

Active prospecting is a rejection-based business approach that doesn't scale. Passive prospecting brings business to you—and it never stops working.

PART 2

PASSIVE PROSPECTING PROCESS

CHAPTER 10

CHANNEL BUILDOUT

Before you start creating YouTube videos, you need to create a home on YouTube where they'll live. How your channel looks and how it's structured will have a significant effect on how easy it is for searchers to find you, the first impressions they form of you, and what they're likely to do next. Whether you end up hiring someone to build your channel out for you or choose to do it yourself, there are steps you can take to maximize your success—and they start at the top.

THE BANNER

Our channel is called Living in Dallas Texas, and if you go there the first thing you'll see is our banner, stripped across the top of the page. It actually tells visitors a lot about us, and yours should too. Take a look, and then we'll break its components down.

 LIVING IN DALLAS TEXAS
16.8K subscribers

SUBSCRIBE

THE TITLE

We didn't pick "Living in Dallas Texas" for our channel title because we liked the way it sounded—although we love the sound of it now. We picked it because it plays a key role in driving our channel to the top of search results for people who want to learn about living in Dallas, Texas.

How do we know? We used a tool called TubeBuddy, an extension for YouTube that you can purchase for a monthly fee. It allows you to play with different titles to see how frequently they're searched—and it even gives you a score and stats on actual searches so your options are easy to compare. (This is a worthwhile investment. In fact, we recommend the Legend version, although it's the most expensive, because of the tools it gives you. We also recommend paying for a one-year subscription upfront, which provides a substantial discount. We'll come back to TubeBuddy later in this chapter and, as you'll see in Chapter 11, we recommend using it extensively when you're deciding on what videos to shoot and how to title them.)

Tool Tip

You can get TubeBuddy at a further discount by going to https://www.tubebuddy.com/TheReelAgents. As of this writing, use the coupon code "andrewsbuddy" for more savings.

You want your title to tell people what they will get from your channel. What can they learn from you? Why should they subscribe? The banner is a value-driven proposition, and the title needs to answer those questions. Make it as clear as day. We don't put our names on our banner; instead, we put "Subscribe to Learn About Living in Dallas Texas." In our industry, most agents display their picture, phone number, and the words "Call to buy, sell, invest." They're making a sales pitch they haven't earned the right to give. There is no value in that. This is the case with any small business. Don't put your website, phone number, and other socials here. Give a clear call to action that displays value for your ideal customer so they are more likely to take action and feel like they are going to get something instead of being sold something.

THE IMAGE

Over our first two years, I made the majority of the videos. Travis was the closer. But you'll see both our images featured prominently on the banner because we're partners. This is all about branding. No one is searching for us specifically, but we want our videos to build a sense of familiarity and relationship with the people who watch them. Putting our photos on there—as big as they can be!—supports that. It helps viewers feel a connection to Travis as well as me, since he is not as visible in most of the videos. I also mention his name in every video so viewers know that the two of us are partners.

Match the background color—and the type, if you can—to your branding. Look closely, and you'll see that we've even got a faint image of Dallas, Texas, in the background, overlaid with blue.

We've also outlined all the visual elements of the banner and given them a shadow. That gives them depth and helps them pop, bringing energy to your banner.

DESKTOP VERSUS MOBILE

The banner displays differently on desktop than on mobile. That's because the screen on your mobile device is smaller. In our case, the mobile screen cuts off at about my shoulder on the left and Travis's on the right. What's outside of those lines—the map on the left, the Zoom invite on the right—only displays on desktop. That means you want the most essential information inside the lines.

We placed the map on the left to paint a visual picture of our business.

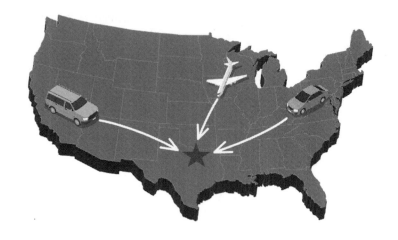

We get a lot of people relocating to Dallas from California, Illinois, New York, Washington, and other distant places, and we wanted to show that we're here to serve those people. It also creates an instant connection. Californians will say to themselves, "There we are, moving in our box truck to Texas." It's a way to build rapport through visual graphics.

Whatever you choose to do with that space, our recommendation is to make it visual.

LINKS

To the right, it says "Let's meet 'in person' on Zoom." We've also got a tease ("New Videos Every Week!") and a big, bold Subscribe link in the center. That's it. Those are the only links you'll find on our channel.

The space to the right is where many YouTubers link to all of their social channels. We don't recommend that at all. You've worked hard to get people to your YouTube page, and it's where you want them to stay. It's the best conversion platform out there. Why would you distract visitors interested in engaging with your long-form videos with other choices on short-form platforms? They're on YouTube because they're in the mindset to watch long-form content; they're there to learn. Once they're on YouTube, you want them to stay on YouTube. Even more important, YouTube wants them to stay on YouTube!

The only reason we want people to leave our channel is to give us a call, shoot us a text, send us an email, or schedule a Zoom call—and we want to make all that very easy. Look at the link: "Moving to Dallas? Let's chat!" On our channel, clicking that link brings visitors to another page with a similar banner to reinforce the familiarity and assure them they're in the right place. We present a simple survey that helps us understand their needs and situation, including their price range and whether they're approved, if they're looking; sellers get another form. We ask for their email and prompt them to schedule a Zoom call.

That's the only reason we would ever want them to leave the channel! The whole goal of our channel is to keep people on the channel, watching our videos until they are ready to give us a call because the time is coming for them to make a move.

THE ABOUT SECTION

Next let's turn to the About section.

LIVING IN DALLAS TEXAS
16.8K subscribers

| HOME | VIDEOS | PLAYLISTS | COMMUNITY | CHANNELS | ABOUT |

SUBSCRIBE

Description

This channel is all about living in Dallas Texas, moving to Dallas Texas, and relocating to Dallas Texas. We also cover living in the Dallas Texas suburbs, moving to the Dallas Texas suburbs, and relocating to the Dallas Texas Suburbs.

If you want to know everything about eating, sleeping, working, playing, the good, and the bad of living in Dallas, Texas, then subscribe▶ and tap the bell🔔 for notifications so you can be the first to know about the current market in Dallas Texas.😊

We get calls and emails everyday of people just like you, looking for help on making their move to Dallas Texas and we absolutely love it.😊 Whether you are moving in 9 days or 90 days, give us a call☎, shoot us a text📲, or send us an email📧 so we can help you make a smooth move to Dallas, Texas. 🏡

📞 Call or Text us: 214-225-6557
📧Email: info@LivingInDallasTX.com
💻Free Real Estate Consultation (Zoom Call):
https://bit.ly/LivingInDallasCall

Stats

Joined Oct 27, 2020

1,430,705 views

As its name suggests, the About section is your opportunity to describe what your channel is all about. Again, it's important to think critically about what you say. Remember, YouTube is a search engine, and it's owned by Google, the world's dominant search platform. YouTube "reads" your words, runs them through its algorithm, and uses the results to determine where you fall in search results. That means your description is *extremely* important. Ours aligns with our channel title and our video titles and content—and it's very literal: we're not worried about repetition. We're worried about matching search terms that people who are interested in living in Dallas, Texas, are likely to use.

If you want to see how much this matters, Google "Living in Dallas Texas" and look at the results. Things can change, but as of July 2022, our Google Business Profile dominated the right side of the first page of search results, all the way to the bottom. It identifies us as a real estate agency and includes reviews, the description, links to free downloads, and our contact information. That's all very powerful. Our videos are also featured prominently in their search results; if you were to click on the Videos or Images tabs, you'd find us there too.

No matter what business you're in, our goal should be your goal: to make it as easy as possible for Google and YouTube to connect your YouTube channel and website to what people are searching for.

One more thing: our Google Business Profile is the only place we link to our YouTube channel. Period. Otherwise, we want people to find us organically. If people are on Google and searching, they're probably signed in to Google and in research mode. We want YouTube and Google to know who they are when they land on our channel, so they can feed them more of our videos.

THE COMMUNITY TAB

The next part of the channel buildout is the Community tab. We treat it like its own social media platform—and we generate a lot of engagement from here.

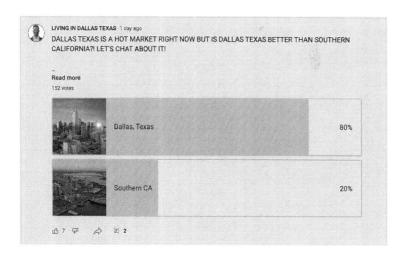

We post lifestyle or neighborhood-related photographs here, occasional Google reviews, photos of food, even photographs of ourselves. They all get good engagement in terms of likes. We post our videos here too—and have found they get the *least* engagement. That's not what people are looking for when they click on the Community tab. Instead, we've found that they're looking for a sense of community and belonging.

This also makes it a great place to stay on top of your community. You can do polls here, asking your audience what videos they'd like to see next. That can only deepen your understanding of what your audience is looking for.

THE PLAYLISTS TAB

We create playlists of videos on related topics—in our case, starting with popular suburbs like Prosper, Frisco, or Plano. We create playlists of our neighborhood VLOG tours, places to eat in Dallas, things to do in Dallas, even the pros and cons of living in Dallas. The same approach works regardless of your business.

HOME   VIDEOS   SHORTS   LIVE   PLAYLISTS   COMMUNITY   CHANNELS   ABOUT   Q   >

Created playlists

Sort by

Living in Dallas Texas #Shorts

Luxury Living in Dallas Texas

Dallas Texas Real Estate For Sale

Living in Prosper Texas

Fort Worth Texas Suburb VLOG Tours

Updated yesterday
View full playlist

View full playlist

Updated 5 days ago
View full playlist

View full playlist

View full playlist

Dallas Texas Neighborhood VLOG Tours

Places to Eat in Dallas Texas #shorts

Things To Do In Dallas Texas #shorts

Dallas Texas Google Maps Tours

Dallas Texas Suburb VLOG Tours

View full playlist

Updated today
View full playlist

Updated today
View full playlist

View full playlist

Updated 2 days ago
View full playlist

111

Once a viewer clicks on your playlist, YouTube will play all your videos in that list, one after another. You're removing ads, suggested videos—which could be from a competitor—and any other distractions. If someone is really interested in your content, they'll stay on your playlist to the very end.

That uninterrupted experience is a great way to foster relationships. We've had dozens of clients tell us that they binge-watched twenty or thirty of our videos before calling. It can happen!

THE CHANNELS TAB

The Channels tab allows you to link to other channels if you want to. We don't recommend it, because you don't want to distract your audience by pointing them away from your content—unless it's to another channel that you've created.

The only external channels we'd consider adding on our Living in Dallas Texas channel would involve a partnership with another creator. In real estate, perhaps it would be a mortgage company; in plumbing or auto sales, perhaps a parts supplier.

We do link to external channels on a second channel we've created, our Passive Prospecting: YouTube For Real Estate channel, because it provides evidence of the other channels we have been able to help and coach them to duplicate the same results and success we have experienced!

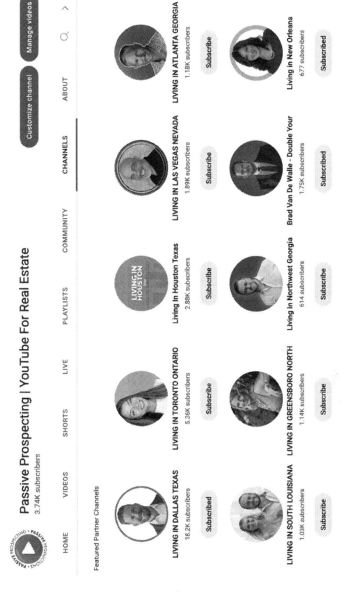

But generally speaking, we think it's best to avoid distractions and keep your audience on your channel.

THE VIDEOS TAB

The Videos tab lists all your videos in chronological order, starting with the newest. You don't have to do anything to populate it; YouTube keeps adding videos as you post them. It's an interesting way to see the evolution in your channel in terms of your topics, thumbnails, and views.

Viewers can sort by oldest and most popular. Don't worry about your oldest videos, even though viewership may be low, as long as they are related to your business. Wear them as a badge of honor that shows how far you've come. Never delete old videos; just unlist them if they are no longer related to your channel.

Note

When you're working with any platform, they may change at anytime—and just as we were nearly finished writing our book, YouTube changed how it handled shorts! You can now clip long-form videos to make YouTube shorts that link back to the long-form version, and shorts are now searchable too. YouTube also added a Shorts tab alongside the others we're covering in this chapter. You'll find a discussion of these changes—and how to approach platform changes in general —in Chapter 14.

SUBSCRIBERS

Some YouTubers don't display their number of subscribers. Don't be embarrassed by a low number. We've displayed our subscriber count from the beginning. Remember: we got our first call about thirty days after launching our channel; we only had forty-eight subscribers, but that didn't stop the phone from ringing. Our Houston team got a call six days after launching their channel, and it was a $750,000 cash buyer. They only had ten subscribers, but they got the call. Kyler and his team closed that deal four months later. Not once was the client concerned with the number of subscribers they had.

Some of your viewers will be proud to stand among your earliest subscribers. When you become YouTube famous, they will gladly tell you they subscribed when you only had 100 or 1,000 subscribers!

YOUTUBE STUDIO AND
YOUR DASHBOARD

When you're signed in to your YouTube account, you should be able to click on your avatar in the upper right of your screen, then pick YouTube Studio from the dropdown menu. That's going to bring you into the backend of your channel, beginning with your channel dashboard. You'll be presented with your notifications, subscriber account, and channel analytics over the past twenty-eight days. You'll also get a look at the performance of your most recent video, compared to your previous videos. It's a great summary of recent activity.

Channel dashboard

Your channel
LIVING IN DALLAS TEXAS

- Dashboard
- Content
- Playlists
- Analytics
- Comments
- Subtitles
- Copyright
- Monetization

Latest video performance

BEST TOUR of Frisco Texas in 2022
| Living in Frisco Texas | Moving t...

First 3 days 16 hours compared to your typical performance:

Ranking by views	1 of 10 >
Views	3.8K ⬆
Impressions click-through rate	6.4% ⬆
Average view duration	6:01 ⬆

GO TO VIDEO ANALYTICS

SEE COMMENTS (24)

Important notifications

Video received a copyright claim

A copyright owner claimed some content in your video, "Living in Desoto Texas Levi Lascsak Dallas Texas Real Estate Agent". Please note:...

Sep 14, 2022, 8:18 AM

VIEW OPTIONS ⋮

Channel analytics

Current subscribers

17,135

+762 in last 28 days

Summary
Last 28 days

Views   70.2K ⊘
Watch time (hours)   7.5K ⊘

117

You'll also see a list of other options down the left side of your screen. Most are self-explanatory.

"Analytics" brings you deeper into the performance of your channel and your individual videos. It's our favorite tab, because it's extremely helpful for identifying trends and understanding the factors that are driving viewership, whether they're recent or since your channel was launched. It's easy to see your top-performing videos in a given period. It puts a detailed breakdown of your views, watch time—an essential metric—and subscribers at your fingertips.

"Content" shows you what's been published, in order, along with what's been scheduled—an important feature that allows you to control when your posts go live. If you find that videos published on Sundays perform best, great! YouTube's scheduling feature will work weekends so you don't have to. "Comments" lets you see and reply to comments in a single place; "Monetization" presents options for monetizing your channel if that's your goal.

"Customization" is an important tool, so we'll look at that in more detail.

CUSTOMIZATION

By clicking on Customization, and then Layout, you customize your channel homepage, beginning with selecting a trailer and a featured video. These appear at the top and do important jobs.

VIEW CHANNEL

Channel customization

Layout   Branding   Basic Info

Video spotlight
Add a video to the top of your channel homepage

Channel trailer for people who haven't subscribed

$3,800,000

Video title
Inside A $3.8 MILLION McKinney Texas Home | Luxury Listing in McKinney Texas | Dallas Texas Su...

Featured video for returning subscribers

Video title
DON'T Move to Dallas Texas | WATCH FIRST BEFORE MOVING to Dallas Texas | Dallas Texas Real E...

Your channel
LIVING IN DALLAS TEXAS

Playlists
Analytics
Comments
Subtitles
Copyright
Monetization
Customization

119

The trailer video plays automatically for those who have not yet subscribed to your channel. It's a prime opportunity to capture their attention. In 2022, when the real estate market reacted to rising interest rates, we highlighted a video with me talking about the market shift—and flipping upside down as I introduced the topic. (Things were crazy and that showed it!)

The featured video greets subscribers every time they come to your channel. It's a different audience, so you should make a different choice—and change both of them out as circumstances and viewership develop. You'll need two videos to fill these positions—and it's important for you to make deliberate decisions about your trailer and featured videos as you add more content. In our industry, most agents post an introductory video. As with self-promotion in the banner, we don't recommend doing this; it's just a sales pitch. We don't feel we've earned the right to talk about ourselves on our own channel. It's value first, always.

The Layout section also lets you select which playlists to display on your channel homepage.

Layout   Branding   Basic info

Featured sections

Customize the layout of your channel homepage with up to 12 sections. Learn more

+ ADD SECTION

≡ **Uploads (144)**

≡ **Popular uploads (144)**

≡ **Single playlist: Dallas Texas Real Estate For Sale (10)**

We put our "Uploads" playlist at the top, which means our most recent videos are featured first. We want to make it easy for subscribers to find our most recent content. From there, we add playlists based on their popularity. In our case, that means playlists from the most popular videos to the most popular suburbs around Dallas; for a plumber, it might mean faucet, toilet, and water filter playlists, and for a financial adviser, different investment options. The opportunities for any business are endless.

Next, we put our most popular videos after the uploads. It's not about vanity, but about making the phone ring. Highlighting the videos with the most views adds credibility to your channel. It's like that little "K" next to your subscriber count; once you hit 1,000 subscribers, it bumps up your credibility that much more. Again, it's nothing to obsess over, but it helps.

You can add new playlists, up to a total of twelve; it's as simple as clicking on "New playlist." Remember TubeBuddy from earlier in the chapter? Here's another instance where it's very useful. Using Keyword Explorer, you can test a variety of options for naming your playlist, just as you did with your channel name itself. Why bother? Because you should think of your playlist titles as search terms.

Let's return to real estate for an example. Say we wanted to create a playlist for our Dallas listing videos. We could simply call it "Dallas Real Estate Listings." Keyword Explorer gives that a score of 74 out of 100, which is pretty good. "Dallas Texas Listings" brings us to 84. But listings is really a term that real estate agents use, and not necessarily our audience. So how about "Dallas Texas Real Estate for Sale"? That hits the jackpot: 100/100. Keyword Explorer tells us that's the search term people are most likely to use, so it's our winner. Then, having titled our playlist and published it, it's just a matter of adding the videos to populate it using the Content feature and determining where it should display in the list of playlists using the Playlist feature.

One last tip: edit the playlist to include a full description of the list itself. More is better; lay it all out. Think of it as a blog post in itself. Why? Because the description is searchable; a full description makes it more likely your playlist is going to be found by someone who is searching for the information your playlist will give them. YouTube wants to make that connection happen, and this is telling YouTube what your playlist is all about.

Dallas Texas Real Estate For Sale

10 videos · 185 views · Updated 2 days ago

Public ⌄

This playlist is all about homes in Dallas Texas, luxury homes in Dallas Texas, moving to Dallas Texas, and properties for sale in Dallas Texas. If you're moving to Dallas Texas, this is the playlist for you!

Dallas Texas homes are what we do, and we want you to be able to see what it looks like and feels like to move to a Dallas Texas neighborhood or a Dallas Texas suburb. This playlist features home tours in Dallas Texas and beyond. Make sure you like and subscribe to the channel to get the latest and greatest from the Living in Dallas Texas team!

If you're looking to buy in the Dallas Texas area, be sure to give us a call, shoot us a text, or send us an email. You can even schedule a Zoom to speak one-on-one with me and the team! We look forward to helping you make Dallas Texas home.

$3,800,000 | 21:09
Inside A $3.8 MILLION McKinney Texas Home | Luxury Listing in McKinney Texas | Dallas Texas Suburb
LIVING IN DALLAS TEXAS

$1,400,000 | 14:59
INSIDE A $1.4 MILLION Dallas Texas Home 2022 | Luxury Living in Dallas Texas
LIVING IN DALLAS TEXAS

$5,150,000 | 18:07
TOUR A $5,150,000 LUXURY CONDO in Legacy West in Plano Texas | Luxury Living in Plano Texas
LIVING IN DALLAS TEXAS

$4,300,000 | 16:31
INSIDE A $4,300,000 Preston Hollow Home in Dallas Texas | Luxury Living in Dallas Texas
LIVING IN DALLAS TEXAS

$775,000 | 10:19
TOUR A $775,000 OLD EAST DALLAS Texas Home | Dallas Texas Real Estate
LIVING IN DALLAS TEXAS

$2,975,000 | 10:50
INSIDE A $2,975,000 Heath Texas LAKE HOUSE | Moving to Heath Texas | Dallas Texas Suburb
LIVING IN DALLAS TEXAS

$3,150,000
TOUR A $3,150,000 HOUSE in Preston Hollow Dallas Texas | Luxury Living in Dallas Texas

---

Branding

The Customization feature also allows you to control your branding, beginning with your profile picture. We recommend having a photo of a single person. Trying to stuff more than one person in a small picture is a lot, and a logo doesn't make the same connection with viewers as a person does. Of course, it's up to you, but that's our recommendation. If you've got a business partner, it's important to set ego aside and recognize that someone needs to be the face of your business on YouTube.

This feature also allows you to upload or change your banner. Remember to optimize it for all devices. You want it to look good on all formats.

A Template You Can Use

If you like our banner, here is a link to the template so you can adjust it to fit your business: https://bit.ly/ChannelBannerTemplate

Finally, you can add a watermark that will display on the bottom of your videos. It pops up after five seconds. You might consider putting a subscribe image down there; if someone scrolls over it, it's going to pop up a subscribe button. If you want to be playful, put a little emoji figure with a big finger pointing up; if someone scrolls over it, that finger will be pointing to the subscribe button. You don't want to overpower the video, but it might pique a viewer's curiosity.

Basic Info

The Customization feature also allows you to change your channel name and description. You can change your channel name at anytime, but we don't recommend doing it very often—and you should always repeat the exercise using TubeBuddy to test the options you're considering.

YouTube does not give exclusivity to channel names. There can be ten "Living in Dallas Texas" channels. Since we've started, we've seen more! If that happens to you, you might want to consider a tweak to provide some exclusivity, but ultimately, you can't prevent others from doing the same.

This is where you can add or change your channel description too—your About section. You're limited to 1,000 characters; we use 988 of them. We always recommend making the most of the space you're given, because it's SEO. As with playlists and video titles, this is telling YouTube what your channel is all about. When people are searching for something you can help with, you want your channel to pop up.

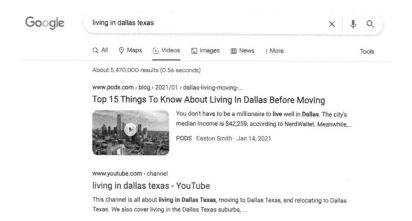

This approach is what allowed us to show up as the Number Two option organically on the Google videos tab when someone searches "Living in Dallas Texas."

URLs and Links

After you get one hundred subscribers, you can create a custom URL for your channel that's easier for viewers to remember. This is unique, even though your channel name is not.

The Customization section also allows you to determine which links you'll display. You can have up to five—but as we said earlier in this chapter, we believe less is more, in terms of keeping people on your channel. Why give your viewers' decision indecision?

VIEW CHAN

Channel customization

Layout   Branding   Basic info

Name

Choose a channel name that represents you and your content. Changes made to your name and picture are visible only on YouTube and not other Google services. Learn more

LIVING IN DALLAS TEXAS

Handle

Choose your unique handle by adding letters and numbers. Learn more

@LIVINGINDALLAS

https://www.youtube.com/@LIVINGINDALLAS

YouTube also just released handles. As of this writing, your handle will be the same as your unique URL, and it makes it easier for others to find and interact with you—so be sure to get to one hundred subscribers as soon as possible!

CHANNEL SETTINGS

In the left-hand column of YouTube Studio, you'll find a link to your channel Settings tab. This is your final stop in completing the buildout of your YouTube channel.

If you click on Channel, you'll see a Basic Info section that includes space for you to list all the keywords you want associated with your channel. These won't be displayed anywhere for people to see, but they're one more way to optimize your channel so it's easy for searchers to find. YouTube allows you up to 500 keywords. We recommend that you make the most of the opportunity, because once again, this is telling YouTube what your channel is all about. Remember: YouTube reads your words! We use 448 out of our 500 keyword limit. All it takes is creativity in thinking through the variations. Once again, you'll find TubeBuddy's Keyword Explorer to be very helpful in finding the best keywords to use.

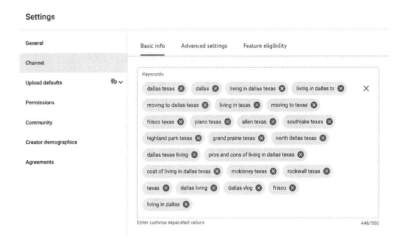

Next, click on Advanced settings. The first choice you'll see there is about your audience; specifically, whether your channel is made for kids. We recommend selecting No—unless your audience is exclusively kids. YouTube puts a lot of limits on channels that are focused on kids, because they're trying to do all they can to protect children on the internet.

Lower down, you'll find the option to display your subscriber count. Again, we recommend displaying the number, no matter how many subscribers you've got. Don't be ashamed of a low number. We believe a low number may motivate people to subscribe if they find value in your channel, because they'll want to help out. They might even feel like they're joining an exclusive club of insiders. If they find value in your channel, they're not going to be scared off by a low subscriber number. Will calls increase with more subscribers and viewers? Absolutely. High numbers only help—but a low number won't hurt.

UPLOAD DEFAULTS

Upload defaults is the most important section in your channel settings, because it controls the defaults associated with all your videos. Let's start with the "Basic info" fields.

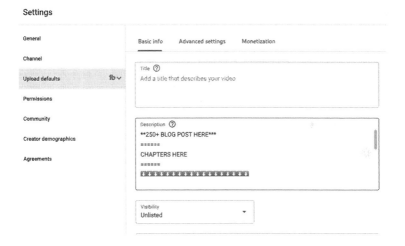

Leave the Title field blank. You don't want the same title on every video; you want that to be custom.

The Description field allows you to create a default description. That's a great place to start—with a standard description.

You can always customize it. On average, we end up writing a 250-word blog post for each video. But we start with a placeholder as a reminder, followed by a reminder to display the chapters in the video (chapters are break points added by an editor; we'll get into those later in the book), and finally our contact information.

Here's why we put our contact info low in the description: as soon as we publish a video, we copy that contact information into a comment and pin it at the top. We can always unpin it later, but this allows us to display both the first three lines of description of the video and our contact information right beneath the video. That means no one has to scroll to find it.

⊚ DALLAS

DON'T Move to Dallas Texas | WATCH FIRST BEFORE MOVING to Dallas Texas | Dallas Texas Real Estate

79,385 views • Premiered May 21, 2021

⚪ 1.6K　🖓 DISLIKE　↷ SHARE　↓ DOWNLOAD　✂ CLIP　☰+ SAVE　⋯

ANALYTICS

EDIT VIDEO

⬤ **LIVING IN DALLAS TEXAS**
16.8K subscribers

Should you really move to Dallas Texas? Today, we'll walk you through the 11 CONS of moving to Dallas Texas! Let's talk about a few of the downsides of living in Dallas Texas today. There are a TON of pros – don't get me wrong. I wouldn't live here if the pros didn't outweigh the cons – but it's worth noting that

SHOW MORE

---

671 Comments　☰ SORT BY

⬤　Add a comment...

⬤　⚲ Pinned by LIVING IN DALLAS TEXAS

　　(LIVING IN DALLAS TEXAS)　1 year ago

　　▪ Call or Text: 214-225-6557
　　▪ Email: info@LivingInDallasTX.com
　　▪ Let's Zoom: https://bit.ly/DallasRealEstateCall
　　▪ Subscribe ✎ ✎ ✎ http://bit.ly/LivingInDallasTexas

　　⚪ 12　🖓　♡ REPLY

　　▸ ⬤ • 7 REPLIES

This also means that YouTube isn't reading our contact information first; that wouldn't tell them anything about our video. We want to give YouTube a full, custom description for each video. Remember, always: YouTube reads your words. Most You-Tubers don't understand this. They just post videos and don't fill in the blanks. We'll say it one more time, because it's important: you need to tell YouTube what your video is about, to help them match your video to searchers looking for the information you're providing.

Why start with default content, if it's likely to change? It saves you time. All you'll need to do is change whatever parts you're customizing for each video.

The Visibility field allows you to determine whether a video is public, private, or unlisted by default. We default to unlisted, because we want to upload the video and then schedule it. You could default it to public, which means as soon as you hit save, then that video's going to be published. We don't recommend ever doing that. You need the opportunity to do your customization work before it goes live, and then schedule it for publication.

Finally, you can add your tags—one more opportunity to help YouTube match your video to searchers. We'll get into that in more detail soon.

ADVANCED SETTINGS

The Advanced settings section provides a few options worth noting.

First, we recommend selecting Allow Automatic Chapters when available and eligible. This will help when it comes to adding chapters to your video, a topic we'll cover in Chapter 12.

Selecting a Category provides one more way to help YouTube bring searchers to you. We defaulted to Education, knowing that our users are researching information about moving to Dallas.

Selecting "Standard YouTube License" is fine.

Under Comments, we recommend selecting "Hold potentially inappropriate comments for review." YouTube is pretty good about capturing inappropriate comments, so this adds a layer of protection without allowing a free-for-all at one extreme or stifling all comments at the other. Neither extreme serves you well.

We also recommend defaulting to yes on "Show how many viewers like this video." As with appropriate comments, people like to see engagement.

MONETIZATION

This section is available only after you've reached certain criteria. As of this writing, it's 1,000 subscribers and 4,000 watch hours within a calendar year. YouTube will let you know when you're eligible.

Once you've crossed the threshold, you gain some control over the ads YouTube displays with your videos, as well as a share of the revenue they generate. We don't do any overlay ads, because we want to keep the focus on our video. We do allow sponsored cards, skippable video ads, and non-skippable video ads. We don't allow mid-roll ads during our videos, even though they make the most money. We're in a fortunate position, because our primary goal isn't making money on YouTube ads, but generating real estate business. The choice is yours. Remember, YouTube will play commercials at the front of your videos and at the end, regardless of your choices, so you might as well make money on those ads.

OTHER SETTINGS

The Permission section allows you to manage permissions by adding managers or editors to your channel.

The Community section relates to live videos. It allows you to designate monitors to review comments, for example, or to write the welcome message participants get when they join. You can block curse words or prevent participants from posting links—all tools intended to make the live video a positive experience for everyone who joins.

We don't make use of the Creator demographics or Agreements sections at all. Again, the most important settings for you to focus on are the Upload defaults.

Channel Buildout Takeaways

How your YouTube channel looks and how it's structured will have a significant effect on how easy it is for searchers to find you, the first impressions they form of you, and what they're likely to do next. Many YouTubers just jump in and start posting videos. But the words you use to describe your channel and your videos are critically important, because they help YouTube put your videos in front of searchers looking for the information you share.

CHAPTER 11

CONTENT CREATION

Now that you understand how to build out your YouTube channel, it's time to turn to the videos themselves: content research and creation, which we'll cover in this chapter. What's true for your channel is true for your videos too. Deciding what videos to make and how to make them isn't a matter of guesswork. It begins with finding out what your customers are searching for, and then putting content that answers their questions in front of them. It's also a matter of mastering the video flow blueprint: understanding how to structure your videos so they work for your audience. Once you've grasped these fundamentals, you'll find you approach producing your videos with a lot more confidence.

DECIDING WHAT VIDEOS TO MAKE

We talked in Chapter 10 about TubeBuddy, the YouTube add-on that helps you determine what search words your audience is using, then lets you test and tweak until you find the very best terms to use. Again, we recommend biting the bullet and paying upfront for a year's subscription to the Legend version. That gives you the best tools at a discounted price. We found this was a necessary expense, because it made it simple for us to figure out exactly what videos to create and how to title them. This is crucial to success. (The Legend version also allows you to do A/B testing, a topic we'll cover in later chapters. Here is the link again in case you haven't downloaded yet: https://www .tubebuddy.com/thereelagents.)

USING KEYWORD EXPLORER

You could just jump in and start making videos on the topics you think are most important to your customers, but we don't recommend it. If you've got a lot of experience in your business, guessing could work—but remember, YouTube is a search-based platform. You don't need to guess; you simply need to figure out the questions your audience is asking, then answer them. TubeBuddy's "Keyword Explorer" lets you do just that.

If you're a car salesman, you'd want to know what questions

buyers are asking *before* they walk onto your lot. For a financial adviser, you'd want to know what investment options or money worries generate the most searches. Is it saving for retirement or paying for a dream vacation?

In our business, most sales involve the suburbs. When we started out, we needed to know which suburbs generated the most interest. Keyword Explorer provided the answers. You can either do a weighted search, which reflects activity on your channel, or an unweighted search. When you're starting out, an unweighted search makes the most sense, yielding the most useful results until you build up enough content to rely instead on the weighted search.

We'll use the Dallas market as an example. Keyword Explorer tells us that the words "Plano, Texas" generate 834,000 searches per month. "Frisco, Texas" generates 640,000. That surprised us. Based on our call volume, we'd have guessed that Frisco was the most popular suburb, but 200,000 searches is a significant difference. It's important to be exhaustive, so you shouldn't stop there. You'd explore every suburb where you wanted to work and keep notes in a spreadsheet so you could rank the results. Prosper, Texas, is a newer suburb; it generated 136,000 searches. McKinney, Texas, generated 558,000 searches. Next, let the numbers guide you.

That means you'd rank the fifteen or twenty suburbs you ended up with from the highest to the lowest search volume.

Then you'd start at the top—Plano, in our example—with one or two videos. Why? Because beginning with the most searched suburb is going to increase the likelihood that your videos will be found quicker. That's going to drive more traffic to your channel. Think about your business and the main topics that will cover the major categories. If you're a financial advisor, maybe it's stocks, bonds, ETFs, index funds, and so on. If you work at a car lot, it could be Ford, Chevrolet, Dodge, etc. You may love Ford, but if Chevy is the most searched car, that means you might want to make videos on Chevy first. If you're a financial advisor, you may prefer stocks, but if index funds are searched more often, starting with that topic will make it easier for you to be found quicker.

CHOOSING YOUR TOPICS AND TITLING YOUR VIDEO

We're not done with TubeBuddy yet. The Keyword Explorer can also help you zero in on what videos to make and how to title them. Let's stick with our real estate example: we've decided to start with two videos about Plano, Texas. What questions are people who are considering moving to Plano likely to have? There are lots of options, and they're all worth exploring: the pros and cons of living there, the most popular neighborhoods, things to do there, how the schools rank, a map tour, a vlog tour. They might even want to know if tornadoes ever strike Plano. But of all these topics, which are the most likely to bring you traffic?

Keyword Explorer helps you test your way to an answer—and

better still, how to lock in on the title that's most likely to drive results. (Again, this approach will work for any business. Say you're a used car dealer, and you've found that Ford F-150s are a top search topic. What questions are people considering a F-150 likely to have? You could guess, but testing with Keyword Explorer will tell you the answer.)

We're going to cut to the chase on our real estate example and tell you what our testing revealed as the top question searchers have about any suburb around Dallas: what are the pros and cons of living there?

That's a great place to start. But how should you title it?

Keyword Explorer tells us that "Plano, Texas pros and cons" gets a search score of 86 out of 100. How about "Living in Plano, Texas pros and cons"? That's a 60. Not nearly as good. But "Pros and cons of living in Plano, Texas" gets an 87. Now, is shorter better? In this case, yes. "Pros and cons of Plano, Texas" gets a 93. How about mixing it up? It turns out that "Good and bad of Plano, Texas" gets a 96. Of these five choices, those are the words people are actually most likely to use when they're trying to answer this question on YouTube—so that's how you should title your video.

These differences may seem small. But as your search volume grows, a 5 percent advantage in one title over another has a compounding effect. It may seem small in the beginning, but it adds up over time.

TubeBuddy also allows you to try your top two choices with an A/B test and see which one gets the best results for you. That's a powerful tool; we use it all the time. And here's another option when two choices stand out: combine them into a long-tail title, such as "Pros and Cons of Plano, Texas | Good and Bad of Plano, Texas".

Remember, whatever your topic, your goal is finding the title that delivers the best results in search. It's worth the time and effort it takes to get your title right, because it's essential for your video to rank as high as possible in search results. As more and more competitors find their way to YouTube marketing, dialing in every aspect of your video will make a huge difference.

One study found that 70 percent of searchers choose one of the top five search results they see. More than 25 percent actually click on the top result. (The tenth result gets 2.5 percent of clicks—and that's not where you want to be.)[23]

The bottom line: you want to rank in the top five search results—always. You *always* want to give your videos the best possible chance of being found.

---

[23] Matt G. Southern, "Over 25% of People Click the First Google Search Result," Search Engine Journal, July 14, 2020, https://www.searchenginejournal.com/google-first-page-clicks/374516/#close.

OTHER WAYS TO RESEARCH CONTENT

You've got options beyond TubeBuddy for researching content. Here's a rundown of several.

Google Keyword Planner: Google Ads offers a free keyword planner. You'll need to create a Google advertising account to utilize it. This tool analyzes Google search traffic, as opposed to YouTube search traffic. We haven't found it particularly useful, because it's YouTube traffic that interests us, but it's a tool you can try.

YouTube search bar: Go to your channel and click on the YouTube search bar. If you were to type in, say, "Plano, Texas," the search results that pop up are very similar to TubeBuddy. This will tell you top results—but without TubeBuddy, you can't tell how many searches there were or optimize your title.

Google: Simply searching your topic on Google will show you results that can be helpful. Look for the "People also ask" section—that's Google telling you these are highly searched questions. Depending on the search term you used, Google might also show you the top sights, stories, news articles, or videos on the topic you're interested in.

Specialty websites: In almost every business field, there are specialty websites that will suggest topics for videos. For example, in real estate, niche.com pulls together data by community on population, median home value, median rent, top schools, top neighborhoods, and more. These are all potential talking points for videos. Ratings on sites like these can give you a way to talk about sensitive topics such as "top schools" or "top neighborhoods" without viewers thinking that you're pushing your opinions. Sites like Yelp and Tripadvisor give user ratings on places to eat and things to do. Wikipedia can be a great resource. Whatever the source is, we make it clear that we're not presenting our opinion, but sharing information in hopes that it's useful. That's because real estate agents cannot be seen as favoring schools or neighborhoods because of fair housing laws. In other cases, though, it's possible your opinion may matter most. AnswerThePublic is another website that provides video topic possibilities for almost any small business.

Once you've produced a couple of videos on each of your most searched topics, from the top of the list to the bottom, you can return to the top and work your way back down with a new set of videos—building out your library of videos for each suburb, pickup truck brand, investment option, whatever your business may be. As you build out, remember to focus on evergreen content, not seasonal. Continue to experiment, test and let the numbers guide you to success. It worked for us, and it can work for you. If one of your earlier videos on a topic starts to take off with views that surpass your average, make an adjustment as soon as you can. You may be planning to shoot several videos on other topics in your business, but if you see an earlier video start to gain momentum, change your plans. See if you can make a follow-up to the earlier video on the same topic to see if you can capitalize on its momentum.

VIDEO FLOW

Now let's get into making the videos themselves, starting with how to structure them. The first thing to think about is your setting. You want something that's visually appealing and relevant to your topic.

In our case, when making a neighborhood video, we always try to start in a spot that's a major draw: in the historic downtown, a park, or a shopping center. We like areas with a little character, in settings that feature cool boutiques, restaurants, and coffee shops. It makes for a good backdrop. For office videos, an artistic background that displays your personality is best. This can be as simple as shelving, pictures, art—or a blurred background, if all you have is dirty laundry back there!

THE HOOK

The first thirty to forty-five seconds of your video is the hook—although it really boils down to the first three to four seconds. Even with long-form video, you've only got so long to capture someone's attention. Because time is of the essence, and the first three spoken components of our video flow—the hook, the call to action, and the social proof—are generally the same, we recommend memorizing them. You can begin by writing these elements down, printing them out, and recording yourself reading them through; then plug in your headphones and play them back, reading your words again at the same time. That will help you refine and memorize them very quickly. We've found that memorizing our openings makes it much easier to flow into the substance of our videos, which aren't scripted.

The hook is very simple: address the viewer, and start with what led them to click on the video in the first place. Using our early videos as an example, our hook would be something like "So, you're thinking about moving to Plano, Texas?" or "So, you're thinking about moving to Frisco, Texas?" If you're a plumber, it could be "So, your toilet won't stop running?" For that car salesman, it's "So, you're thinking about buying a Ford F-150?"

We start with a question because we want people to say yes or no. If they say, "Yes, I am thinking about moving to Plano, Texas," they're likely to keep watching. If they say, "Actually, I'm not thinking about moving to Plano, Texas, I want to move to Frisco" and jump off, that's okay. That tells YouTube they're not interested in more Plano content. If they search Frisco, Texas, and one of your videos pops up and they start watching, that tells YouTube to send them more of your Frisco videos instead.

When circumstances change, it's important to consider adjusting your hook. Although our initial "thinking of moving to Dallas Texas" opening generated a lot of relocation clients, we later began to see more and more local calls. We didn't want to alienate local clients, so I made a change. Now I start out by saying, "So you're thinking of buying (or selling) a home in Dallas Texas"—an opener that works for local *and* relocation clients.

People make decisions quickly. If you look at our analytics on a typical video, you'll see a sharp curve, beginning with an early drop. About twenty-five to thirty seconds in, about a third of the viewers have stopped watching. They dropped off early. Again, that's okay. The ones who matter most to your business are the two-thirds who stay.

It's also important to remember that your hook does double duty. It also tells YouTube what your video is about. YouTube transcribes what you say in your videos and feeds that into its algorithms to deliver your video to the people you're trying to reach. That means your hook helps YouTube position your video.

Having framed the question—"So, you're thinking about moving to Plano, Texas?"—here's where we typically head next: "Well, in this video, we're going to take you around Plano. We're going to show you three different homes at three different price points. That way you can get a good idea of what may fit inside your budget. And if you stick around until the end, we're going to share with you one of the hidden gems of Plano that not a lot of people know about—so you don't want to miss out on that. We're going to get after it right now."

And that is our hook. It takes thirty to forty-five seconds. We use that time to tell viewers—and YouTube—exactly what they're getting in that video.

ANCHOR MUSIC

From there, we play our intro music. It only takes about six seconds, and we don't recommend you go above that. A lot of YouTubers will tell you that you don't need this, and you should do what you feel is best. But we think of that little snippet of intro music as an anchor that helps brand our videos.

Think about it. Anytime you hear the *Friends* theme song, you probably think of *Friends*. The same goes for *Seinfeld*. Why did their producers bother with theme music? Because it's iconic. It's branding that anchors the show in your mind. When you hear the *Seinfeld* jingle, you associate it with the show, and it lets you know what's coming. I would also bet that almost no one can identify the artist or the name of either song; instead, they'd just identify it as the *Friends* or *Seinfeld* theme.

To us, the shorter the better. Four to six seconds is really ideal. We've seen YouTubers with ten, fifteen, even twenty-second intros, and we want to tell them, "Stop it! Don't do that." At a certain point, the music becomes a distraction—even an annoyance. Keep it short and sweet.

THE CALL TO ACTION

The viewers who are still with you want to be with you, so it's time for your call to action. Again, this is memorized. We imagine a brand-new audience member, and we give them a reason to subscribe. "Hey," we'll say, "if this is your first time on the channel, and you want to know everything there is about living in Dallas, Texas, then subscribe below and tap the bell for notifications so you can be the first to learn about the current market in Dallas."

We do that for several reasons. First, we want to connect with that new viewer and keep them on our channel. To achieve that, we have to give them a reason why: "Go ahead and subscribe below so you can be the first to learn about the current market in Dallas." We don't worry about aggravating regular viewers; they know we're going to say it.

Here's a pet peeve: please don't ever say, "Subscribe so that you know every single time I drop a new video." Put yourself in the viewer's shoes. If they're new to the channel, imagine the questions they'll have: "What are you going to be talking about? Are you just going to try to sell me something, or are you here to help me understand my choices?"

When we say "be the first to learn" it creates an insider feel. It makes it clear that subscribing to our channel will keep them up to date on the current market, and that we are the team to do it.

Viewers will identify with whoever is making the video, so if you're alone on camera but are working as part of a team, make that clear—because when someone calls, you don't want them to be surprised if they get someone other than you. As we built out our business, I made the videos, and Travis closed the deals, but he rarely appeared on camera; we made certain to mention Travis's name in our call to action. Now we work with a large team, and we make that clear too.

SOCIAL PROOF

Next we offer social proof, demonstrating that we are here to help and that viewers respond: "We get calls and texts every single day from people just like you looking to make their move to Dallas, and we love it. Whether you're looking to move in nine days or ninety days, give us a call, shoot us a text, send us an email, or schedule a Zoom call. We're happy to help you make that smooth move to Dallas." While we're saying these words, we'll pop a couple screenshots of texts we get or us being on Zoom calls to prove the point.

This is memorized too, and we choose our words carefully. Why the nine to ninety days? Because we want people to know that it's never too soon or too late to give us a call.

I remember one of the first clients we got under contract. They had been in Dallas for four days working with a different agent. They felt that the agent wasn't listening to their needs, and they only had one day left in town. The night before that last day, they went on YouTube hoping to find an area in Dallas they hadn't been to yet. Several of our videos popped up. They watched them all and emailed us that night at eleven.

I woke up the next morning, saw the email, and waited until 8:00 a.m. to call them. After a conversation, I recommended a new community that had everything on their wish list. We agreed to meet there at lunchtime. A few short hours later we had them under contract on their ideal home. It fit all of their needs and was going to be finished for them to move in perfectly in three months. When I asked why they had called, and at the last minute, their answer shocked me: "We called because you said whether you're moving in nine days or ninety days!"

Never underestimate the impact of your call to action and the words you choose!

We spell out the choices for reaching us—a call, a text, an email, or a Zoom call—because different people have different communication styles. If they reach out by text or email, we know that they're likely to be readers and writers. If they call, they're probably auditory people who want to hear your voice. If they want to Zoom with us, they're kinesthetic-type people. They want to see us to get to know us better.

The way people reach out to you the first time is a huge indicator of their communication style, and it tells you what they're likely to be more comfortable with as you proceed. No matter what business you're in, you always want to meet people where they're at. You want to go to them; you don't want to sit there and try to drag people into your way of doing things.

SUMMARY AND SUBSTANCE

From there, you want to summarize what you have to say, beginning with where you are—"So here I am in the historic downtown district of Plano, Texas, and what I love about this area is…"—and then get into the meat of what you have to say: "Now we're going to go through some neighborhoods, and we're going to check out a $300,000, a $600,000, and a $1 million property so you can see some homes that may fit your budget."

That tour makes up the bulk of the video. It's where we get into the nitty gritty of answering the questions our viewers have: how does Plano look and feel, and what will my money buy there? Can I picture my family being happy there?

Once we're into the substance of the video, we're just talking, as if we're in a conversation with the viewer. We wouldn't memorize anything more than the bullet points we want to cover.

This is easier than you might think. And we say that knowing that 75 percent of Americans rank public speaking as their number one fear—ahead of death, which is crazy![24] Many people are just as uncomfortable about getting on camera. The more you do it, the easier it becomes. Business people have conversations with customers all the time, and eventually it comes naturally. All you're doing is telling the camera the same things you'd tell that customer if they were standing next to you. The key to getting comfortable on camera is remembering that you're much more critical of yourself than anyone else. Most people will simply admire you for taking the time and effort—and having the courage—to do it.

RECAP

Your video should tell a story, and stories need an ending. We like to finish up with a brief summary, then restate our call to action: "And remember, whether you're moving in nine days or ninety days, feel free to give us a call, shoot us a text, send us an email, or schedule a Zoom call—and until next time! We hope to show you around town." Again, keep it simple. What you're trying to convey is, "Hey, I want to work with you. Come on over for a visit, and I'll help you out."

---

[24] Pat Ladoucer, PhD, "What We Fear More Than Death," MentalHelp.net, https://www.mentalhelp.net/blogs/what-we-fear-more-than-death/.

If you're in a different business than real estate, of course, the particulars of where you are and what you cover will vary. But the flow we're outlining will work for any business.

DURATION

Ultimately, a video should be as long as it needs to be. Don't leave out information if it's important, but don't over-talk just to extend the video. Our typical community vlog tour takes between twelve and fifteen minutes. The shortest has been about ten minutes; the longest, twenty-five to thirty. Focus on the question or questions that led your viewer to your video, and answer them. Whether that leads to a short video or a long one, let it be.

OFFICE VIDEOS

Sometimes there's no escaping sitting at a desk and recording an office video. The flow is no different, but the circumstances are. Here are some things you should think about if you want to produce a professional, engaging result.

First, you don't need fancy equipment or a videographer to do the shooting. In general, we recommend a selfie stick that doubles as a stand, a microphone, and a smartphone that has a wide angle lens. (For iPhone users, that means an iPhone 11 Pro or up; the first Android phone with a wide angle was the LG G5.) You typically won't need the wide angle lens for an office video, because the focus is on you, but it's essential in the field, where you want to show as much of your environment as possible.

Before filming, simply put your phone on your selfie stand and position it horizontally.

VISUAL DEPTH

To shoot an effective office video, you want to be in the foreground with a background that provides a sense of depth behind you. The more depth the better. It quite literally gives your video dimension and visual interest, without distracting the focus from you. It's a great way to display your personality. We also like to add an element that's moving, such as the light stick you can see in the corner of the following image. Its colors change in a regular, rhythmic pattern. That gives your video dynamism.

People often ask if the image you see was shot with a green screen. The answer is no. That's our office!

CAMERA POSITION

The camera should be at eye level or slightly above. You don't want to be looking down at the camera, or to have your neck crunched at all, especially if you're wearing your microphone. You want to be looking straight ahead or up just a bit, because then your voice will project a little more.

CAMERA SETTINGS

Your camera should be set to a frame rate of sixty FPS (frames per second) at HD 1080p, or high definition. We don't recommend filming in 4K; it'll take up all the storage on your phone, and it's going to be extremely time consuming to transfer it onto a Google Drive or Dropbox, and then for your editor, if you're working with one, to download it as well.

Shooting in HD format at 1080p yields a sharp image. The sixty frames per second frame rate makes it easy for the editor to speed up or slow down the footage.

FRAMING

In most cases, I like to be framed from the bottom of my shoulders to the top of my head. The main reason for that is eye contact.

You want to fill the frame, so that you appear as close as possible to the camera. You won't use the wide-angle lens for a shot like this. (But if you're sharing the screen with a partner or want to convey the full expanse of your background, the wide-angle lens will do the job.)

I also believe it's important to be open to new learning. I've noticed that a lot of successful creators film from the waist up, including their hands in the frame. As I researched this, I discovered they may do this because nonverbal communication accounts for at least 70 percent of your message's impact.[25] We talk with our hands! This may help hold a viewer's attention

---

[25] Jacq Spence. "Nonverbal Communication: How Body Language & Nonverbal Cues Are Key," Livesize.com, https://www.lifesize.com/blog/speaking-without-words/.

during longer videos. I plan to experiment with this strategy in future videos.

If you're sitting, sit straight up; if you're standing, don't sway. If you've got an office chair that swivels, sit still. (It's better to avoid a swivel chair if you can, because that makes it harder to fidget.) You don't want to rock back and forth. When you're filming, you want to be as locked in and professional as possible.

We always recommend the back side of your camera for filming. Most people use the front side, so they can see themselves as they film—even though the camera lens on the front side is off to the side. If you're looking at yourself on the screen and not the camera lens, it'll appear as if you're looking off to the side on your video. You'll never make eye contact with your viewers, and that makes it very difficult to establish a connection with them. It's as if you're afraid to look them in the eye.

Looking into the lens on the back side of your phone eliminates that distraction. It forces you to make eye contact with the camera itself—and that gives you eye contact with viewers.

That said, for filming office videos, it's probably easier (especially at first) to use the front camera to make sure you are properly positioned in the frame. Just remember to look at the camera lens, not yourself! In the field, using the wide angle lens, you'll never have to worry about being in the frame.

BE CONSISTENT

If you're publishing evergreen content, *when* you publish your videos doesn't matter very much. Remember, it's intentional marketing; your videos simply need to be there whenever your viewers are ready to consume them.

But *how often* you publish your content does matter. We've found that once you reach twenty videos on your channel, that's when your viewership typically jumps up. If content is king, consistency is queen—especially in the beginning. You have to create a consistent flow of good content to transform your business.

We recommend filming a month's worth of content before you begin publishing. If you're going to post two videos a week, film eight; if you're going to publish three videos a week, film twelve. You want to begin with a buffer, because if you don't, life happens—health happens, family happens, and then possibly nothing happens. Publishing only a couple videos followed by a gap will kill your channel quicker than anything else.

Then you need to figure out a flow for filming more content that's nonnegotiable. It might be one weekend a month—four vlog videos, out in the field, on a Saturday, and four office videos on a Sunday. The point is to block out the time it takes to film your videos and stick to it. If someone wants to meet or talk during your video time, tell them you've already got an appointment. We've never had someone say they won't do business with us because of a previously scheduled appointment. Making your video time nonnegotiable is the best thing you can do for yourself.

YOU CAN DO IT

Now you know how to research and title your videos, and you have a sense of how to structure and shoot them. Don't over-complicate this. The sooner you start using YouTube videos to build your business, the better.

You don't need to research every last word you say, and you don't need to script your entire video. You don't need to be perfect, either. These are *your* videos, your content, and they're reflections of you.

For the most part, you just need to talk to the camera, as if someone sat down next to you and asked you a question. What you say should come from your experiences, your stories, and your expertise. What the research can give you is ideas and talking points—details you don't necessarily have at your fingertips the first time you do a video.

It's also important to know that you don't need to record your video in a single take. If you're doing an office video, you can talk to the camera, stop, look at your notes, talk to the camera, stop, look at your notes, back and forth. If you stumble badly, just stop and start over. You can trim the content you don't want in the editing process, whether you're doing it yourself or working with an editor. That's just a question of how best to leverage your time.

It's easier than you think. The most important thing to remember is to make eye contact with the camera lens—and be yourself.

Your videos are a way to consolidate every conversation you've ever had with a client on a topic over the past two, three, four, five, ten, or twenty-five years. The difference is that you're having that conversation on camera, not over a cup of coffee at a diner. But video conversations don't end when you leave the diner; they last forever, waiting to be found again by the next searcher with questions you can answer.

Videos are simply conversations at scale—and nothing is more powerful than that.

Content Creation Takeaways

Deciding what videos to make and how to title them shouldn't be guesswork. TubeBuddy can show you what your audience is searching for and how to title your videos so they'll be found. Making videos is easier than you think. The key is to make eye contact with the camera—and to be yourself.

CHAPTER 12

OPTIMIZATION

YouTube employees who work closely with content creators have told us that every single video lives individually on YouTube. This is important. If you publish a video that does extremely well, that doesn't guarantee your next video will do well too. On the other hand, if you publish a video that does poorly, it won't tank your channel.

Because every YouTube video creates its own opportunity, every one of your videos needs to be optimized individually to give it the best chance of being found by searchers and promoted by YouTube. We can't emphasize this enough. Making the best video in the world won't make a difference for your business if searchers can't find it.

That means your work is not done when you film and upload your video. You need to take advantage of every opportunity

YouTube gives you to maximize its success. Our philosophy is if YouTube gives you a blank box on the back end, it's there for a reason; fill it in.

Optimizing is a time-consuming process, which means it may not be the best use of your time. You can hire an editor who specializes in this work to do it for you, as we have. (In fact, we've actually built our own editing team—and they're available to help you too.) But whether you optimize your own videos or hire help, it is important to understand the basics of how and why it works.

You'll optimize your video in YouTube Studio, YouTube's backend interface, which you access on your channel. It's where you set all your defaults when you build out your channel. (We covered that in Chapter 10.) If you've got TubeBuddy, that's a bonus. It's integrated into YouTube Studio, and it will help you step by step as you optimize several key elements of this work, testing as you go: the title and description, tags, and thumbnails.

At the end of this chapter, we'll include a link to reach our editing team, if you're looking for help.

But first, let's walk through the key elements of optimizing your video.

FILE NAME

Before you upload your video, change the file name to match your key search terms. As you can see in the example, we included the name of our channel, the person featured in the video, and another keyword phrase. (It's in the lower right corner of the following image.) This won't display to viewers, but it will help your search ranking.

Video details

Test Alternates   UNDO CHANGES   SAVE

Title (required) ⑦

Living in Cedar Hill Texas 2022 | Next Dallas Texas HOTSPOT? | Moving to Cedar Hill Texas

89/100

Description ⑦

Are you thinking about moving to Cedar Hill Texas? Let's walk through Cedar Hill Texas and see the bang you can get for your buck here!

Cedar Hill Texas is really a hidden gem in the Dallas Texas area! It's a small, quaint town now, but it's quickly grabbing the attention of people all over the Dallas Fort Worth area. Homes are reasonably priced, and living in Cedar Hill Texas means being close to other larger cities with some of the extra amenities most people enjoy being close to. It really is a great area!

There are some great spots to eat here in Cedar Hill Texas, including Babe's Chicken in Cedar Hill Texas. You definitely need to stop in here and grab some of the best comfort food in the area here! Today, I'll take you around to three different homes in three different price ranges so you can get a feel for what fits inside your budget. Cedar Hill Texas is really an awesome spot to look if some of

Video link
https://youtu.be/IOI2f44W-I0

Filename
Living in Cedar Hill Texas - Levi Lascsak Dallas...

Living in Cedar Hill Texas - Levi Lascsak Dallas Texas Real Estate Agent.mp4

168

TITLE

Your file name will also be the default title on your video once it's uploaded. The file name helps tell YouTube what your video is about; we're optimizing that for internal purposes. Searchers see the title, not the file name.

We recommend changing the title to match the terms searchers are likely to use. For that reason, we recommend using the keyword twice in your title. (Remember, TubeBuddy can help you identify your keywords.) Here's an example:

Video details

🔵 Test Completed ~   UNDO CHANGES   SAVE

Title (required) ⑦

Living in Southlake Texas 2022 | AMAZING SUBURB in Fort Worth Texas | Moving to Southlake Texas

95/100

Description ⑦

Are you thinking about moving to Southlake Texas? Let's explore Southlake Texas today! Southlake is a great place to live for families and professionals alike. The city offers top-rated public schools, plenty of job opportunities, and a wide variety of recreational activities and amenities. If you're looking for a safe, comfortable place to call home, Southlake is definitely worth considering.

If you're looking for a luxurious, spacious home in a safe and family-friendly community, Southlake is the perfect place for you. The median home price in Southlake is about $1 million, but there are plenty of homes available at all price points. Whether you're looking for a sprawling estate or a cozy starter home, you're sure to find something that suits your needs in Southlake. Southlake is also home to a variety of businesses and job opportunities. The city's proximity to

Video link

https://youtu.be/IJpEXvzYXNM

Filename

Living in Southlake Texas - Levi Lascsak Dallas...

Living in Southlake Texas - Levi Lascsak Dallas Texas Real Estate Agent.mp4

You'll notice we don't have any punctuation in the title. If you were writing a letter or addressing an envelope, you'd put a comma between Southlake and Texas. But think about it: When you search something on Google, do you actually add punctuation and use proper grammar? We doubt it, and we want our title to match what searchers type. In addition, the comma may actually make it more difficult for YouTube to "read" your title, and that can hurt your search ranking. This isn't guesswork; we've found that keywords that don't have punctuation perform better than those that do.

DESCRIPTION

As you can see in the following image, we've added a 250-word blog post to the description, specific to this video, replacing the default description we created as a placeholder while building out the channel. In this case, you can see that we've used our keyword—Keller Texas—three times in the first three sentences, and we've done it without a comma. These are simple sentences, and that's okay. We want to make it as easy as possible for YouTube's algorithm to read the description.

Video details

Title (required) ⑦
Living in Keller Texas 2022 | Moving to Keller Texas | Fort Worth Texas Suburb

78/100

Description ⑦
Are you thinking about moving to Keller Texas? Let's explore Keller Texas today!
There are plenty of things to do in Keller Texas, whether you're looking for outdoor fun or indoor activities. For those who enjoy being active, there are plenty of parks and trails to explore. Keller also has a variety of shopping and dining options, so you can always find something new to try. Keller Texas is close to Southlake Texas. Keller is served by Keller Independent School District and Keller ISD schools are highly rated. Keller also has a variety of private schools to choose from. Keller Texas is a great choice for residents who don't want to pay the premium prices in Southlake Texas, but has many of the same amenities and conveniences of living in Southlake Texas.
If you're looking for a city that has it all, Keller Texas is the perfect place for you. Come see why Keller is such a great place to live!
If you're thinking about moving to Keller Texas, or anywhere else in the Dallas Texas or Forth Worth Texas areas, be sure to give us a call, shoot us a text, send us an email, or schedule a Zoom call. We'd love to help you make a smooth move To Keller Texas!

If you're using TubeBuddy, its "SEO Studio" feature can rate your title and description and offer tips for improving it. You need to strike a balance here. Overusing your keyword in a clumsy way, intended to game the algorithm—that's keyword stuffing—will actually lead YouTube to penalize your search ranking. Here's an example of keyword stuffing: simply typing Keller Texas Keller Texas Keller Texas three or more times in a row. You need sentences or phrases that actually make sense and are relevant to a reader, even if they're so simple they read like they were written for a fourth-grader. Don't repeat the keyword in every single sentence either. That's why we space out Keller Texas in the body of the description.

As you can see, our use of Keller Texas got a perfect score.

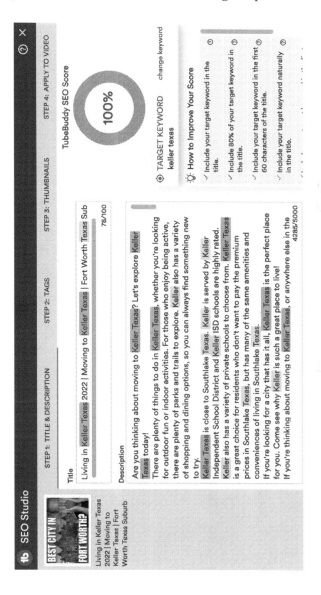

We recommend writing your description outside of YouTube, which makes it easier to check its length. You can copy and paste it into YouTube when it's ready.

TAGS

YouTube allows you to add keywords up to a total length of 500 characters, and our recommendation is to use at least 400 characters. You want to make the most of every opportunity YouTube gives you to optimize the chances your video will be found. Here, again, TubeBuddy is a big help, offering you suggested tags that you can sort and add with a click of a button.

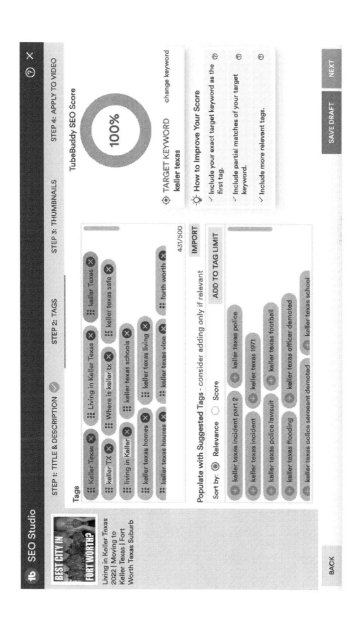

Ideally, your keyword should be your first tag. The additional tags we look for first are partial matches: Keller TX, Living in Keller, Keller Texas Public Schools. From there, we add other keywords—so long as they're relevant to our searchers. (Again, beware of keyword stuffing! YouTube is cracking down on this practice.) Adding these variations maximizes the chances of your video being found.

One more great thing about YouTube: if you've already made a video on the same topic—in our case, say, a suburb—then you don't have to do your tags from scratch all over again. YouTube lets you reuse those tags in your new video. (For that matter, you can use the same title and description if you want, but we don't recommend that.)

THUMBNAILS

Thumbnails matter. They display in search results and on your playlists—so they're the first thing searchers see as they decide whether to click on your video. They're fun to make, even if you've got no editing experience, and especially if you use the right tool. We recommend Canva, a free graphic design tool that comes with a preloaded YouTube thumbnail template, set to the right dimensions. (There's also a Pro version with more capabilities, available for a fee.)

Having said that, if you don't have design experience, we

don't recommend creating thumbnails yourself. It's not the best use of your time. If you're working with an editing team, they'll create them for you.

But if you want to experiment—or create an alternative thumbnail for A/B testing using TubeBuddy—then Canva can make creating the thumbnail simple.

A thumbnail has three basic components.

A background image. Select something relevant to your video content. We've found that making the colors more saturated—again, you can do this in Canva—gives it a more dramatic feel. Because we're in real estate, we usually go with pictures of homes, parks, popular streets, monuments, or other well-known landmarks.

A head-and-shoulders image of you, or whoever is featured in the video. Remove the background, so it's simply your head and shoulders—you can do this easily in the Canva Pro edition with the background remover tool—and then make yourself uncomfortably large! Seriously. The viewer needs to see the whites of your eyes. You want your face to take up the majority of the space, from top to bottom, wherever you've positioned it against the background. We almost always put ourselves in the far right corner; the timer showing the video length displays in that corner, and it helps draw the eye. Use Canva to create a white line around your image so that it stands out, separating it from the background. We like using the glow effect. Make sure your picture does not take up more than one-third of the space on the thumbnail.

Text. Keep it short, simple, big, and bold. Play with the color of the text to find something that stands out against the background and complements its colors. Add a little shadow to the words so they pop. We recommend no more than three words. When you're really good, your thumbnails can have no words if your image can tell a story without text on it. Your thumbnail should be clickbait! But not in a sense that it doesn't match up with your video content. There is a difference between clickbait and bait and switch. The catchier the better; as we know curiosity killed the cat, and drama is always of interest to people. We don't recommend making every thumbnail negative, although negative words or expressions do draw a crowd. Try to balance it out with positive content and happy faces!

That's it: you've created a simple thumbnail.

Here TubeBuddy is useful again. First, once you've uploaded your thumbnail and associated it with your video, TubeBuddy lets you compare your thumbnail with others that are relevant and already posted on YouTube, whether they're your videos or a competitor's.

As we've said, TubeBuddy also makes it easy to run an A/B test on your thumbnail and an alternative. It'll switch out your two thumbnails every other day until one demonstrates a statistically significant higher click-through rate. You can stop the test at anytime and go with the winner—or try another alternative and test again.

CHAPTERS

Chapters are sections within your video that you identify, like chapters in a book. They are individually searchable, creating another opportunity for optimization. They'll also make it easy for people to navigate through your video.

You'll see channels within a video pop up in Google searches, and they will display at the bottom of your video too. We also place a list of chapters in the description, because that's one more way to create customized, searchable content.

areas, be sure to give us a call, shoot us a text, sen
you make a smooth move To Keller Texas!
======
00:00 - Intro to Keller Texas
01:22 - About Keller Texas
06:07 - House #1 in Keller Texas
08:32 - How to Purchase a House in Keller Texas
10:57 - House #2 in Keller Texas
13:14 - House #3 in Keller Texas
15:04 - Wrap Up on Keller Texas
======
⬇️⬇️⬇️⬇️⬇️⬇️⬇️⬇️⬇️⬇️⬇️⬇️⬇️⬇️⬇️
😀Thinking of Moving to Dallas Texas? 👑

We recommend doing at least five chapters on a video—even if it's a really short video. Just look for segments that you can identify. We've tested and found that the best place to place your list of chapters is just below the 250-word description. We set them off with separators, such as stars or lines, so it doesn't appear as one big block of words to the viewer.

When it comes to keywords, chapters are their own animal. You can repeat the same keyword in every chapter, because each chapter will rank on its own in Google. It won't hurt you to use the same keyword—Keller Texas in our example—for every chapter. In fact, you should *always* incorporate keywords into your chapter titles.

Again, though, no keyword stuffing! That's simply a bad practice. Make sure your chapter label is actually relevant to that portion of the video. You can even do a Google search for the FAQs on your topic, and lean on those in writing your chapter titles. Relevant titles create a better viewer experience and boost your watch time, and YouTube will reward that by showing your video to more people. If viewers have a bad experience with the chapters because you label them as something that they're not, just for the sake of keywords, they're going to leave the video.

Again, you can write your chapters outside of YouTube, then copy and paste them in. Be mindful of the format: the timestamp is always four characters. That means it's not 3:30, but 03:30. (Obviously, after ten minutes, it's just 10:00.) Otherwise, it won't register with YouTube as a chapter, so it won't turn into a link that takes viewers to that part of your video. Always start with 00:00 as your first chapter.

FIXED CONTENT

After all the content in our description is individualized, we include our fixed content. These are upload defaults, because they're going to be the same for every video.

This begins with our contact information. We place it as close to the top as possible, right below the individualized, searchable content. We set it apart visually with arrows so it stands out. If a viewer's on mobile, this will stick out like a neon sign.

⬇️⬇️⬇️⬇️⬇️⬇️⬇️⬇️⬇️⬇️⬇️⬇️⬇️⬇️⬇️⬇️⬇️⬇️
🙂Thinking of Moving to Dallas Texas? 🤠
📝 Let Us Help! https://bit.ly/MovingToDallasSurvey
📱 Call or Text: 214-225-6557
📧 Email: info@LivingInDallasTX.com
📅 Zoom: https://bit.ly/LivingInDallasCall
⬆️⬆️⬆️⬆️⬆️⬆️⬆️⬆️⬆️⬆️⬆️⬆️⬆️⬆️⬆️⬆️⬆️⬆️

Below that, we have links to partners, our Subscribe call to action, and our default description. This matches the content in the About section of our channel, which helps tie individual videos to our channel. That's one more way to help YouTube match your videos to searchers looking for the answers you can provide.

We also include our free value offerings, such as a link to a utility concierge and a moving checklist. (We don't require people to enter their email addresses or phone numbers to download these resources; again, it's about service. And we have no interest in chasing people. We want them to come to us, but only when they're ready to make a decision.) We also include our licensing information and the required legal disclaimers and notices.

HASHTAGS

At the very bottom, we have hashtags—two of them custom, specific to the individual video, then three of them anchor hashtags, which are defaults, the same on every video. The anchor hashtags don't actually display; they're in the background, where they'll still help with your search ranking. The custom hashtags do display, so they're the most important. That's because searching by hashtags is becoming more popular on YouTube.

Again, you can use TubeBuddy to test your choices. A total of five to seven hashtags is best practice—but if you think more would benefit the video, add them after your anchor hashtags. They won't display, but they will help your ranking.

PLAYLISTS

You can add your video to multiple playlists on your channel, but you want to start with the most relevant. Again, this will help YouTube steer searchers to your content. Your video will also display with others in the same playlist. Playlists are searchable on YouTube as well, which is why it is important to write the descriptions for them as we suggested in the Chapters section.

VIDEO LOCATION

Populating the Video Location—where the video was shot—is very important. That's obviously the case in our business, real estate, but it's relevant for any video. You can even narrow it down to neighborhoods. We highly recommend this if it is relevant to your business.

Recording date and location

Add when and where your video was recorded. Viewers can search for videos by location.

Recording date	Video location
None	Keller

END SCREEN

You have the option of adding an end screen that displays at the end of your video. Some YouTubers just fade off, but we see the end screen as an opportunity for engagement. Our end screen is the same across all our videos, and we keep it simple: a background image and a Subscribe button, then "Best for Viewer," a choice that lets YouTube recommend a next video from our channel that its algorithm suggests is best for the viewer. You could also add a link to a playlist in your channel, but we believe it's best to give the viewer just one option. As we've said before, we don't want to create decision indecision.

Your end screen can be between five to twenty-five seconds long. Ours runs on the short side, because we've found that converts at a slightly better rate. (It's all about testing!)

PIN YOUR CONTACT INFORMATION

After your video is published, we recommend copying your contact information from the description, pasting it into a comment, and pinning that comment to the top of your feed. That means your contact info will be prominently displayed to a viewer whether they click to see your full description or not. The easiest way to do this so you never forget is to publish your video as unlisted. Then you can click the link to "watch it on YouTube," where you are the only one viewing it. Simply pin your comment as the first comment. Go back to the studio and schedule the publish date and time. When the video is published, your contact information will be right there, potentially bringing searchers to you, from the moment your video begins getting views.

> ## Looking for editing help?
>
> Remember, our editing team is available to work for you too. Here's how to get in touch: https://passiveprospecting.com /video-editing-services.

YOUR EDITING TEAM

If you've hired our editing team, or chosen another one, then they'll do all of this for you, every single video, every single time. All you have to do is shoot the content. In our opinion, it's a worthwhile investment, because it lets you focus on the work only you can do.

Still, it's important to understand how optimization works. This is a skill worth developing—because you never want to be completely dependent on your editing team. You want to be able to check their work, and you can't do that without grasping the mechanics and importance of how optimization works. It will also help you understand why your editing team does what it does. We've had clients who tried to change all of our optimization settings because they didn't complete our course, so they didn't understand our strategy.

Optimization Takeaways

A great video won't boost your business if searchers can't find it. Using every opportunity YouTube provides to optimize your video is well worth the time and effort it takes, but it may not be the best use of your time. An editing team can help.

CHAPTER 13

LEAD CONVERSION

Our good friend Amanda Doll says, "If you have to do anything twice in your business, you need a system, process, campaign, or an automated trigger so that you never have to do it more than once yourself." It's great advice, and our experience shows why.

At the time Travis joined me and became our deal closer, we were already having between a dozen and fifteen clients coming into town to find a house every month. And it was already getting really hard to keep track of them. When it's June or July and someone tells you they're coming into town in August, if you don't put it in your calendar immediately, it's easy to forget.

We couldn't have that. And when your passive prospecting campaign on YouTube begins bringing you quality leads, no matter what business you're in, you're going to face the same challenge we did.

After all, bringing in quality leads is only the first half of the battle. Converting those leads into paying customers is the second half—and to do that at any volume, you're going to need Customer Relationship Management software (CRM). Whether you're working on your own, with a small team or a big one, without a CRM, you'll be overwhelmed.

There are lots of CRMs out there. We've developed a customized system that meets our needs called the ReelCRM. It's optimized for our business workflow, and we make it available to real estate agents who take our Passive Prospecting course in YouTube marketing. (You'll find a link to learn more about what we offer in the Conclusion.) It's taken us a year and a half to build it out, piece by piece. As our team has grown, it's become more complex. It will always be a work in progress!

We use our CRM to track where leads are in the conversion process—the sales funnel that leads from first contact to a signed contract. As our leads move through the funnel, the CRM automatically manages a lot of the communication. It's no substitute for the human touch, but it's become an essential tool in building the relationships that lead to sales.

Our advice is to start simple, beginning with picking up a pencil and piece of paper and mapping out your sales funnel. What are the steps that a customer needs to take to get from contact to conversion? Here's an example of what we're talking about:

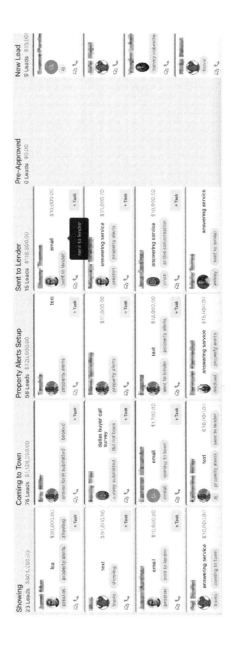

You'll want to structure your CRM to follow that flow. The specifics will vary based on your business, but you can think of it as involving three basic steps: contact, conversation, and conversion.

CONTACT

When a new client decides to contact us, they've got four options. (Remember, that's the power of passive prospecting. We don't chase clients; clients come to us.)

One is clicking a link to schedule a Zoom call. That actually brings them first to a survey. Buyers get a survey that captures the information we need to help them find the house they're looking for: their budget, time frame, the type of house they want, whether they're pre-approved, and so on. Sellers get a different survey: address, square footage, time frame, what they think the value of their house is, and more.

We'll focus on the buyer side in this example. But either way, capturing this initial information when they're ready to act sets them—and us—up for success. It also brings them into our CRM automatically. After they book a Zoom consultation, they'll end up on a thank-you page that directs them right back to YouTube: "Hey, thank you so much. You're all set. Someone on our team's going to be reaching out to you here shortly. Go ahead and check out our latest video."

We also get inbound phone calls, text messages, and emails that we handle manually. Either way, we bring every incoming client into our CRM.

The steps in our sales funnel are represented in a series of columns in our CRM, beginning with "New Leads" and ending with "Closed." If an incoming client books a Zoom call, Travis—who handles our initial Zoom calls—gets a text alert and the call is entered in his calendar. But we don't want any of our messages to look like they're coming from a bot. It'll come from Travis and read like this: "Hey, Mark." (We get their first name through the survey, so we can personalize our messages from the start.) "Glad to see you scheduled a Living in Dallas consultation. I sent you an email with the Zoom link for our meeting, but here it is again, just in case. And I also sent you a calendar invite to drop the date in your calendar."

If a new client doesn't book a Zoom call, our CRM assigns them to an agent in a round-robin that evenly distributes the work, while also letting us steer high-end clients to our most experienced and successful agents. (We base that distinction on the price value of the home they tell us they're looking for.) When a new lead comes in, and it's tagged to a specific agent, they'll get an automated text message on their phone saying, "Hey, you got a new lead."

When agents get a new lead, they'll respond within an hour.

Moving a client from one column to the next is largely a manual process too—but each step triggers a campaign: a series of automated text messages that help us stay in touch, deepen our relationships, and lead our clients through the sales process.

Every interaction between the agent and the client is captured in the CRM. The agents enter their notes on every conversation in the CRM. That means every step of the way, we're learning more about our client—and making a record of it.

CONVERSATION

We want our initial interactions to provide as much value as we can. If it's a Zoom call with Travis, he's going to have the MLS real estate listings pulled up, and he uses the call to build a customized search list based on what the client is looking for. His goal is dialing in as closely as possible to everything the client wants. He'll confirm whether or not they're pre-approved. If not, he'll also stress the importance of working with a local lender—we work with a preferred mortgage broker—because we want our clients to be pre-approved before they come to town and go through a series of showings. We want them to come ready to buy. That's one reason our time from contact to contract is far faster than the norm.

We rely on our CRM to keep conversations alive. If a buyer

is coming to town in forty-five days, an agent will have a lot of people to talk to between now and then. It's easy to lose track—and you don't want to go forty-five days without talking or touching base without someone coming from out of town. So we'll send a series of automated reminder messages.

Three weeks out, they'll get the first: "Hey, what's going on? This is Levi. I know you're coming into town in three weeks, and I'm super excited. Is there anything that you need help with in preparation for your trip coming into town?"

Two weeks out, they get another text. "Hey, what's going on? It's Travis. I was just thinking about you. Just wanted to touch base. We're super excited to see you. I just wanted to touch base and see if there's anything we can do to help."

One week out, it's the sales agent. "Hey, this is Vince. I'm just checking in. I know you're just a week out. We're so excited to see you. Is there anything we can do to help you prepare for your trip?"

If they respond to any of our messages, we're alerted so we can reply manually.

And finally, just before they come into town, another message from the agent is sent: "Hey, you're just a couple of hours away. Just wanted to make sure you know that I am 100 percent prepared for your trip." When that text message goes off, we've instructed our agents to call the client to make sure they have their list of homes they really want to go see.

CONVERSION

The clients who are in town and in the Showing column are our hottest leads. These are people who are actively looking, ready to buy right now. Let's say they're in town for a three-day visit. We'll set the expectation upfront that they should spend the first day driving all over the city on their own, checking out their top twenty to twenty-five listings, the neighborhoods, the communities, and the schools. We want them to narrow their list.

On the second day, we'll usually only show six to eight homes. Most of the time, because of how much information about their priorities we've captured along the way, that's enough for them to find one that they love. Then we can spend that third day submitting offers and making sure we secure a deal. If they don't find a home they love on the second day, the agent will show them another six or seven homes on day three.

Once the deal is struck, funded, and closed, we move them into the Closed column. That brings them into a final messaging campaign, because we want to thank them and get a review. This is why we have so many five-star reviews. As soon as the buyer's card slides over to Closed, it generates an automated text: "Hey, congratulations again on your closing. We sent you an email about helping us out with a review. If you've already left one, thank you so much. If not, could you help us with a quick review?

We'd really appreciate it." The email gives them instructions on how to find our Google page and leave a review. We don't drop the conversation there either; we'll stay in touch for the first year, checking in occasionally to see how things are going. After all, our clients may choose to buy or sell again.

Of course, not every client who enters our system in the New Lead column ends up in Closed. People get busy; maybe they're a long way out from a purchase and don't necessarily want to be talking to an agent. That brings us to the Ghosted column. It triggers one of our favorite campaigns, because it's literally pulled clients back from the dead.

When you get a new lead, we tell agents to follow up with them at least once a day for the first five to seven days. If they haven't responded by then, we move them into Ghosted. That triggers a series of occasional messages to keep the conversation alive. It does work—and our CRM does the outreach for us, freeing us to spend more time with the clients who are ready to buy.

We move clients we've been in touch with for six months or more to Active Conversations. This is a two-year campaign to reach out to them monthly and keep them engaged. We use a variety of texts and emails to keep the conversation alive, letting them know we are still here for them when they're ready.

KEYS TO SUCCESS

Don't overthink it. Keep your workflow and your CRM simple until you decide that you want to grow your team, and then add more complexity as your team needs it.

Our CRM system is always evolving, but it started simple. You don't need or want a complex system, with elaborate websites or any other features where people just get lost.

We don't drive our clients to a fancy website. We bring them into our CRM. We use it to collect their information as fast and fully as possible. We create all our messages within our CRM, complete with images and buttons. Clients complete their surveys and book their Zoom calls in our CRM. It's optimized for mobile too, so it's easy to use no matter what device they're on.

Don't neglect the human element. Your CRM can shoulder a lot of the work involved in bringing a client along, but there's no substitute for genuine, personal interaction. The CRM allows you to read every message from a client, and you shouldn't try to automate every reply. Make sure that you and your team respond to clients quickly, professionally, and effectively.

Keep things moving. Never leave a client's card in a column unless you want them to be there. Remember, each column—meaning each stage in the sales funnel—has an associated automated campaign. If a client gets pre-approved but the agent doesn't move them on to the next column, the system will continue to send occasional messages to try to re-engage them in the pre-approval process. The last thing you want is for your client to get a random text message that's off the wall. People don't like that.

Get the big picture. If you bring every client into your CRM, the statistics it generates will be invaluable. Here's an example of what ours reveals.

	Page Views		Opt-Ins	
	All	Unique s	All	Rate
> ☑ Start	447	269	-	-
> ☑ Buying Survey	135	93	20	21.51%
> ☑ Selling Survey	41	30	7	23.33%

As you can see, in a month's time, 269 people came to our initial "Contact Us" page, where they were presented with the buy or sell survey. Of those, ninety-three initiated the buyer survey and twenty booked a strategy call with us after completing it. That's a 21 percent conversion rate!

The stats can also help you highlight opportunities for improvement. About one-third as many people—thirty—initiated the seller survey and seven booked a strategy call after completing it. That's a conversation rate of 23 percent. Not bad, but there's always room for improvement. This is a side of our business we're still developing. We only recently started doing seller surveys, and this tells us we still have work to do to dial them in.

Roll up your sleeves. No one held our hand and built out our CRM for us. We've spent lots of time, energy, and effort in the past year and a half building out our funnels, laying out our campaigns, and figuring out when to trigger messages.

If you're in real estate and you choose to work with us, we can provide you with the benefit of all that work by sharing our CRM system.

If your company is big enough, you can hire someone to build out your CRM for you. After all, most of us aren't tech gurus and help is easy to find. You shouldn't have to pay too much for it either.

But in the end, big or small, no matter what your business, it's your system. You need to know it like the back of your hand. For the most part, building it out isn't complex; it just takes time—and the results can be amazing.

The first thing you really need to worry about is getting your YouTube channel up, bringing leads in, and building out your main funnel. Start with a pencil and paper. Take it one step at a time. You only need a handful of campaigns and triggers to get started.

That's all we had for a long time, and we sold a ton of real estate. Our experience shows that you just need to get started.

Lead Conversion Takeaways

Once your YouTube marketing begins generating quality leads, a CRM will become an essential tool in guiding customers from contact to conversion—and doing it at scale through automation. Just start simple and build from there.

CHAPTER 14

ADJUSTING TO CHANGE (AND YOUTUBE SHORTS)

Platforms change. They always will, because they're trying to survive and thrive like any other business. In that sense, YouTube is no different than Instagram, TikTok, or Facebook. (Or Twitter. Just ask Elon Musk!) That means you always need to be monitoring what YouTube is up to and thinking about how to adapt your channel in response. (The same goes for any other platform you use.) In our experience, the key to making the most of any platform change is being strategic in your approach and testing your ideas to see what actually works and what doesn't.

I'll use a big change that YouTube's been rolling out as I wrote this book as an example: YouTube shorts.

YOUTUBE SHORTS

YouTube introduced Shorts—videos of sixty seconds or less—in 2021, our first full year. At first, it felt like the wild, wild, west of Shorts. It was actually a challenge to figure out what qualified as a Short, where they'd end up, or how people would find them. I worried that they'd clutter our channel, and wondered whether they'd get pushed out to the right people—people who were searching for answers about Dallas real estate because they were moving here. When I jumped into chat rooms for discussions with YouTube creators and influencers, everybody seemed to have a different opinion about how to take advantage of Shorts. It just wasn't clear what to do.

I didn't see any evidence suggesting we should abandon long-form content for short-form content—and I still don't. Long-form videos have delivered awesome results for us, for the reasons we described in Part 1 of this book, and they still do. I continue to believe that long-form content is king—at least when it comes to conversion, which is what every business is after. You can't do any better than the king of conversion!

But I also believed that ignoring Shorts would be a mistake. I was curious, and I'm also a big believer in testing. That goes for long-form videos too. At one point we tried posting three, long-form videos at once—a vlog tour, a map tour, and a pros and cons, all focused on one neighborhood. After all, people binge new seasons on Netflix, right? Would the same thing happen if we released a series on a single neighborhood? The answer was ... not so much. One video would take off, but the others died— at least until search began delivering the results we'd always seen. That experiment failed, but at the same time it reinforced our belief that consistent posting of quality content is the best approach. That was good learning.

We took the same approach to Shorts. We knew the only real way to find out whether Shorts would work for us was to experiment with our own channel. After all, it's your own experience that ultimately matters. But we didn't just jump in willy-nilly and start throwing Shorts out there.

Running an experiment takes commitment if you want valid results. I couldn't just post a Short or two and watch what happened. (Remember, if you treat YouTube like a hobby, it'll pay you like a hobby. If you treat it like a business, it can pay you like a business.) I decided to post at least one Short a day for thirty days. As you know, we repurpose a lot of our long-form videos by chopping them into nuggets, or reels, for Instagram and Tiktok.

But we made fresh videos for our YouTube shorts test, in part because if we decided to keep doing them, we wanted to have developed a different format for them. I also wanted them to have utility for our clients, so if I stopped making them after the test, they'd still be relevant.

We decided to focus on two main streams of content for the Shorts: things to do in Dallas, and places to eat in Dallas. I kept it very simple. In fact, you could do it yourself right now; just Google your city or go on Yelp and you'll find Top 10 lists of all kinds. I used those lists as a starting point, and I referenced the source, making it clear that I was simply passing along information from this or that website. Top 10 Mexican restaurants in Dallas, Top 10 barbecue restaurants, Top 10 parks, Top 10 things to do with kids—I just kept them coming. After making one a day for thirty days, I'd end up with fifteen videos on things to do in Dallas and fifteen videos on places to eat. I figured those would have lasting value for clients. If nothing else, we'd create two playlists, and we'd incorporate them into our "welcome to town" emails for out-of-town clients coming in to look at properties.

Here's what happened: we got to about twenty-two days and stopped because the results were already clear. Almost every video I made flatlined for an hour or two, then hockey-sticked to 500 to 1,000 views for an hour, then flatlined again, deader than a doorknob. At the time, YouTube was simply placing Shorts in what they called their Short feed—basically no different than what you'd get if you jumped on TikTok or clicked on the reels button on Instagram. They weren't searchable. That made them nothing more than distractions.

The results showed that our YouTube Shorts weren't reaching our ideal market: people who were actually interested in buying or selling Dallas real estate. We didn't see an uptick in calls, messages, or subscribers. The Shorts didn't affect us positively or negatively. There was no point in continuing the test, especially because it did seem to me that they were cluttering our channel as we posted them.

But then, just as we were finishing this book, YouTube changed the game again.

YOUTUBE CHANGES THE GAME

Late in 2022, YouTube released two significant updates.

First, it allowed content creators to clip Shorts directly from their long-form content, simply using their phones. I've tried it, and it's easy. That Short links back to your long-form video—and that's important. Before, if you wanted to link a Short to a long-form video, you had to put the link in the description and make a reference to it.

Second, YouTube made Shorts searchable. That means they now show in search results for people who are looking for answers.

That got my attention. I checked the analytics on my Shorts—and sure enough, in the previous couple weeks they had all taken off. Every one of them. Over the previous twenty-eight days, we'd gotten an additional 5,000 views from our Shorts, because they were resurfacing as search-based content. I went to YouTube using an incognito window, searched "best Indian food in Dallas," and sure enough, my Short popped up within the top three search results.

▶ YouTube

best indian food in dallas

✕   🔍   ➔   ⋯

‡‡‡ Filters

6:38

Indian Food Like Never Before - Made In Just 5 Minutes

Ad · The Cumin Club Inc

Meal Kits Delivered. Starting at $4.99/meal

Visit s

🔊 SHORTS

The BEST INDIAN Food in Dallas #shorts Places to Eat In Dallas

4.9K views · 1 year ago

 LIVING IN DALLAS TEXAS

FTC Legal Disclaimer - Some links found in the description box of my videos may be affiliate links, make ...

To me, that's a game-changer. If I make a Short that goes mini-viral in the first couple hours just because it's thrown into people's Short feed, that doesn't do much for our business. Is it more brand awareness? Yes. More exposure? Yes. Is it reaching people who are looking to buy real estate today? Probably not.

But if a Short shows up in the search results of someone looking to learn about Dallas real estate, that video could be the introduction that draws them into our channel. That's different. If you think about it, people who are planning a trip to Dallas to look at real estate need to eat too, and they may be looking for things to do while they're visiting. If they've got kids who play sports, they might want to know about the Top 10 High School Sports Districts; maybe they value diversity, and want to know The 10 Most Diverse Suburbs or Neighborhoods.

There were other changes too, and specific limits to consider. YouTube Shorts need to be sixty seconds or less; some argue for fifty-eight seconds to be on the safe side. They need to be vertical in orientation. YouTube has actually restructured how they show on desktop, so you no longer see the black bars of death on either side. You no longer have to include the hashtag #shorts in the title. If you check our Living in Dallas Texas channel, you'll also see that YouTube has separated Shorts (and Lives) with tabs that display below the header, along with About, Community, and Playlists. (You may have to refresh to see the new display.) That means someone on your channel can click Shorts and see every Short you've published. If shorts are what someone is most interested in, they're now easy to find.

I'll be honest: this is a recent change, and we're still thinking about how best to take advantage of it. We're already producing three, long-form videos per week, and that consistency matters. I also don't believe posting one Short per week is going to have a huge impact. But what would happen if we published two or three Shorts every day that we're not publishing long-form content? Two Shorts per day every day? What if we did a week's worth of Shorts in one day once a week? (We could have fun with that: Saturday is our "Shorts day," and we post at 8:00 a.m., 10:00 a.m., noon, 2:00 p.m., and 4:00 p.m.!) You could also clip directly from your long-form video two to five Shorts the very next day. That's like deploying several different "trailers" to bring more attention to your long-form video.

There are lots of options, and with a well-established long-form channel that delivers awesome results, we're taking time to think through how best to take advantage of YouTube's changes. You can be sure that we'll run experiments to test our ideas.

If you're just starting a YouTube channel based on the principles and practices we've shared in this book, you may want to consider incorporating Shorts as part of your passive prospecting business plan from the start. If you've got a well-established channel, you should still always be open to change. Just be deliberate about how you approach it and let the results of your experiments lead the way.

Adjusting to Change
(and YouTube Shorts) Takeaways

As YouTube Shorts make clear, platforms change, and you need to consider changing with them. Just be strategic, test your assumptions, and let the experiment's results lead the way.

CONCLUSION

THE CHOICE IS YOURS

Passive prospecting has changed our lives. After laying out its principles and the process that can lead you to YouTube success, we hope we've shown how it can change yours too.

The team we've created in less than two years in real estate now involves fifteen agents in Dallas alone. We've built an editing team that makes the most of our efforts and frees us to do what we do best. That's enabled us to help others with their editing needs as well. Now Travis and I have the time it takes to share the power of passive prospecting through speaking engagements with audiences across the country—and we have the time and the means to enjoy life too. Not long ago, Travis actually closed six deals while he was on the beach!

We wrote this book to give you all the knowledge you need to launch your own passive prospecting program through YouTube videos. But if you want help, we are ready to support you through the consulting and editing services we now offer.

We're Here to Help

Here's where you can learn more about us and our services: https://passiveprospecting.com.

If you're a real estate agent and would like to partner with us, go to: https://passiveprospecting.com/partner-with-us.

Get our CRM with our funnels and campaigns included for real estate agents: https://thereelcrm.com/.

If you're a small business owner and want our full video course to walk you through the entire process to build and optimize your own channel: https://passiveprospecting.com/small-business-course.

In the end, it comes down to this:

What do you believe?

If you believe that your life and your business are right where you want them, then you can choose not to change a thing.

But if you're not where you want to be, we believe it's just because you haven't learned something yet.

We also believe that when you find that one thing, you can hyper-learn any subject in sixty days. The author and life coach

Jay Shetty says if you read five books on one subject, you'll be more proficient than 99.9 percent of the population on that subject. And whether you want to be proficient on YouTube, Facebook, or Instagram, or if you want to be the best postcard marketer or cold caller on the planet, there are books, videos, and blogs out there just waiting for you to find them. Remember, sixty days is all it took for me to lock in on YouTube and develop our passive prospecting strategy.

Finally, we believe that if you take massive action focused on that one thing, it will completely change your business. We did just that, and it changed ours.

The bottom line: you are only one decision away from changing your life. Once you make that decision, you have to follow it up with massive action.

The choice is yours. Remember, it comes down to what you believe. And we believe since you read this book, you will choose massive success over mediocrity—starting now!

Keep in Touch!

Now that you are committed to passive prospecting and building a life of freedom through video, tag us @levilascsak and @travisplumb with a selfie holding this book and say, "I'm In!"

We look forward to seeing your channel and hearing of your success!

If you'd like to book a free consultation with my team to see how we can help you, scan the QR code below.

ACKNOWLEDGMENTS

FROM LEVI LASCSAK:

I would like to first thank God! He knows I thank Him every day but it is important for others to know I believe in Him and rely on His guidance.

I want to thank my parents, Thomas and Debbie Lascsak, for being my #1 fans, always believing in me, and supporting me in my career choices.

Thank you to one of my best friends and business partner, Travis Plumb. You are the best closer I have ever met and inspired me to go big and realize we always had an earning problem versus a spending problem!

Thank you to my original mentor, Michael Reese. You started me on my personal development journey by taking me to my first event with Brian Tracy. You have always seen I was destined for more and always challenged me to think differently, find a solution, and be the best at everything I do.

Thank you Krissy Owens, the Wizard of Oz! You know how important you are to me and the team and you have been with me through the bad and the good. I could go on and on how critical you have been to our business but that would be another book! :)

Thank you Giselle Ugarte for giving me my first speaking opportunity in Atlanta, Georgia. We went from those one hundred people to 6,000 just one and a half years later!

Thank you to the Real Estate All Day crew (Juan, Christopher, and German) and family. You have welcomed me on your platform over and over again. You are all a great group of people and true to the core.

Thank you to Benji Travis and Sean Cannell for including our story in YouTube Secrets and being more than mentors, but also great friends.

Thank you to Pete Vargas, Brent Gove, Justen Martin, Buck Wise, Brian McCauley, and Ryan Serhant for being tremendous inspirations and coaching us to high levels of success!

Thank you to the entire Living in Dallas Texas Team!

Finally, thank you to my best friends Russell Creamer and Jess Green. Only you two know how far we have come and how we all could have been on different paths. Thank God we are all great at what we do now and that we are still friends thirty-five-plus years later!

—Levi

FROM TRAVIS PLUMB:

I would like to first thank God, who has been with me every step of the way! I praise Him for his strength and guidance in all things.

I want to thank my parents, Leslie and Arthur Plumb Jr., for being my No. 1 fans. You have always believed in me and supported me in my career choices.

I am beyond thankful for my loving wife, Sam, for being there for me no matter what. Through the good times and the bad, you have always been at my side. Having you and our beautiful baby girls is the single greatest gift God has ever blessed me with. Lilah and Scarlett, I love you every minute of every day.

Thank you to one of my best friends and business partner, Levi Lascsak. You are one of the greatest guys I have ever met. A man of God, honest, loyal, incredibly hard working and disciplined. It is an honor to be working side by side with you. You changed my life in more ways than you even know.

Thank you to the entire Living in Dallas Texas team! We wouldn't be here without each and every one of you. This was and will always be a team effort.

Finally, thank you to my best friends, Vincent Morris III and CJ Obsivac. It's been a crazy journey, boys. You know better than anyone just how far we have come. I am blessed by and grateful for your brotherhood.

—Travis

ABOUT THE AUTHORS

LEVI LASCSAK and **TRAVIS PLUMB** have much in common beyond achieving breakout success together in Dallas real estate by following the passive prospecting process they explain in this book.

Both were raised in small Texas towns. Levi grew up in Stephenville, a country town about one hundred miles south of Dallas—a town, he jokes, where there's not much to do besides milk cows, ride bulls, and play high school football, as he did, under the Friday night lights. Travis was raised by adoptive parents in Mesquite, about fourteen miles east of Dallas, where he played soccer and ice hockey growing up. (That's right, ice hockey in Texas!)

Both are combat veterans of the war in Iraq, where Levi served for a year as an Army sergeant and Travis for two, ten-month tours as a Navy Seabee. Both ran gun trucks that provided base camp security and conducted patrols. Levi's duties also included serving in a quick reaction force, while Travis's responsibilities included protecting the Secretary of Defense and the Secretary of the Navy during their visits to Iraq.

Both experienced physical and emotional challenges in the years after their military service. Levi returned home with a digestive disorder, which led to the loss of fifty pounds in one month in 2013, leaving him bedridden and disabled. Traditional treatments prescribed by a series of four gastrointestinal doctors failed to turn things around, and he credits God's grace for leading him to a natural doctor who changed his diet and added supplements that gradually led him back to good health. For Travis, the darkest days involved his mental health, coming in 2018 after a partner embezzled money from their business and left him broke, with one young daughter, Lilah, in the house and another, Scarlett, on the way, unable even to put Christmas presents under the tree. He awoke one morning, lost in self-destructive thoughts, before realizing that Lilah was lying next to him in bed. It was a turning point. "What am I doing?" he said to himself. "Get up and get to work—and thank God for everything you do have."

Both experienced a series of business successes, due to their determined effort and sales and marketing skills, as well as failures due to forces beyond their control, from partners who proved untrustworthy to health issues and COVID-19. Levi's business experiences included pharmaceutical sales and financial services; Travis's included car sales and digital marketing. It was hard work, and sustained success eluded them. Both still loved sales—but they hated prospecting.

Levi and Travis met in the fall of 2020 at the house of a mutual friend, Michael Reese. They soon realized they shared one more thing: a determination to take control of their own futures by building a different kind of real estate business, based on the principles of passive prospecting. Their partnership—along with their friendship and their business—have all flourished.

Made in United States
Orlando, FL
25 April 2023

32425232R00137